WILDFLOWERS OF NEW YORK

IN COLOR

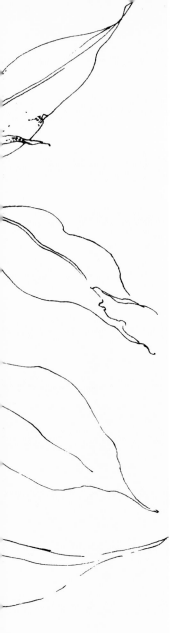

WILDFLOWERS OF NEW YORK

IN COLOR

William K. Chapman
Valerie A. Chapman
Alan E. Bessette
Arleen Rainis Bessette
Douglas R. Pens

Botanical Drawings by
Philippa Brown

Syracuse University Press

First Edition 1998
01 02 03   6 5 4 3 2

This book is published with the assistance of a grant from
the John Ben Snow Foundation.

All photographs by the authors.

The paper used in this publication meets the minimum require-
ments of American National Standard for Information Sciences
—Permanence of Paper for Printed Library Materials,
ANSI Z39.48–984. ∞™

Library of Congress Cataloging-in-Publication Data

Chapman, William K.
     Wildflowers of New York in Color / William K. Chapman,
          Valerie A. Chapman, Alan E. Bessette, Arleen Rainis
          Bessette, Douglas R. Pens
          Botanical drawings by Philippa Brown.
               p.   cm.
          Includes indexes.
     ISBN 0–8156–2746–7 (cloth: alk. paper).
      — ISBN 0–8156–0470–X (pbk.: alk. paper)
     1. Wild flowers—New York (State)—Identification.
     2. Wild flowers—New York (State)—Pictorial works.
     I. Chapman, William K., 1951–   .
     97–29901
     QK177.W55   1998
     582.13'09747—DC21

Preceding page: Bottle gentian, *Gentiana clausa*

Book design by Cristina Lazar

Manufactured in Hong Kong

To wildflower lovers everywhere, with appreciation for your enthusiasm, curiosity, and joy in discovery

CONTENTS

ACKNOWLEDGMENTS

The authors wish to acknowledge the many people who have contributed valuable time and effort on behalf of this book. We are indebted to Richard S. Mitchell for his generous support in providing expertise and advice in reviewing the manuscript. *The Revised Checklist of New York State Plants* by Richard S. Mitchell and Gordon C. Tucker served as our primary reference source for nomenclature and terminology. Our sincere thanks to Charles Atkinson, George Beatty, the late Howard Bradley, Philippa Brown, Evelyn Greene, and Charles Sheviak for assisting us in locating selected wildflowers and for other contributions. Doug Pens wishes to extend his personal acknowledgments to his wife, Eileen, for her constant understanding and support and to Professors Eugene Waldbauer and John Gustafson for their encouragement throughout the years. We thank Bettie McDavid Mason for reviewing the manuscript and offering valuable suggestions for improving the text. We wish to thank Philippa Brown for providing the botanical drawings, and we are especially grateful to Dr. Robert Mandel and his staff at Syracuse University Press, who made this book possible.

HOW TO USE THIS GUIDE

We have prepared this field guide to make identifying unfamiliar flowers as easy a process as possible. By following the simple procedure described below, you will be able to identify the wildflowers described in this book in a matter of minutes simply by making choices having to do with a few easily differentiated characteristics.

The first characteristic to consider is *color*. Is the flower white, the color that is in reality the reflection of all other colors? After white, the other choices are the colors of the rainbow. This guide follows the example of nature and lists those colors in the same order that they are displayed across the sky after a storm, beginning with red and continuing through violet. Within the spectrum, the color that is somewhat problematic and causes the greatest concern is purple. Purple flowers with a predominant bluish cast have been included in the blue to violet category. All the species whose color appears to have been visibly influenced by any degree or shade of pink-to-red pigmentation have been included in the pink-to-red category. The final color choice encompasses the darkest colors to be found on flowers, those ranging from deep purple to brown. Occasionally a flower is found that is such a dark shade of purple that it first appears to be nearly black. However, we are not aware of any truly black wildflower.

One final note on identifying flower colors: In some flowers the color of the petals or the petal-like parts differs from the color of the disc or center of the bloom. In such cases, we have assigned that species to a color category according to the color of the petals.

After you ascertain the color of a wildflower, your next task is to examine the *physical structure of the flower*. Is the flower radially symmetrical or nearly so? Radially symmetrical flowers have petals or petal-like parts that extend outward from the center of the flower more or less evenly in all directions, as in the daisy for example. (The term "petals or petal-like parts" is used throughout this guide to refer to any floral—usually colorful—parts that appear to be a petal, even though technically these parts may be sepals, modified bracts, etc.) If a flower is radially symmetrical, you should then count the number of petals or petal-like parts. The possible categories range from 3 to 7 or more petals or petal-like parts. A few species, such as goldthread or bloodroot, typically exhibit variation in the number of petals per bloom. In these cases we have relied on personal experience in assigning such species to the category that is most appropriate.

Following the 5 categories of radially symmetrical flowers is the final possible selection, a catch-all classification for any wildflowers not fitting into the previous categories. Flowers in this grouping do not appear to be radially symmetrical. They may have fewer than 3 petals or petal-like parts; or flowers that are minute, filamentous, tubular with no or uneven petal-like lobes; or with no obvious petals or petal-like parts. If a flower is tubular to dish-shaped with a number of conspicuous, symmetrical, petal-like lobes, then that species will be found in the radially symmetrical category. If the flower is tubular but the lobes (or "teeth") are either unequal in size and shape or minute, then that species will be found in the asymmetrical category.

After you determine the color and structure of the flower, your next task is to examine the leaves. The leaf arrangement on the plant should fall into one of the following categories: (1) aquatic*, (2) leaves lacking, (3) leaves basal, (4) leaves alternate, (5) leaves opposite or whorled.

In some species leaf arrangement may include two categories, such as having both basal and alternate leaves on the same plant. In these cases the plant is assigned to a category according to which leaves appear to be the more prominent. You should also take leaf arrangement to mean the way the leaves would appear at first glance to the average person encountering the plant for the first time. For example, several species have trailing or subterranean stems that put up leaves and flowers at intervals. If the leaves of such plants appear basal, then that is the category in which they are included.

For ease in identification, each category of leaf arrangement is subdivided by leaf shapes. Leaves can be simple or shallowly toothed or lobed, or compound, or so deeply divided as to appear compound.

To identify an unfamiliar flower, you must first determine the color of the bloom. Flowers within each color category are subdivided according to the

---

*Although "aquatic" is not a true leaf arrangement, it is a useful category for simplifying the identification process.

number of petals, in the case of radially symmetrical flowers, or according to the asymmetrical appearance of the bloom. Turning to vegetative characteristics, you can further narrow the number of choices by identifying the leaf arrangement and shape. At this point you should have only a few species to choose between, and we hope that a quick comparison of the photographs and the accompanying descriptions will provide the correct identification.

PART ONE

WHITE FLOWERS

❧

FLOWERS SYMMETRICAL, WITH 3 PETALS OR PETAL-LIKE PARTS

LEAVES BASAL, SIMPLE

Arrowhead, Wapato
• *Sagittaria latifolia* Willd.
• Water-plantain family **Alismataceae**
FLOWERING SEASON: July–August. FLOWERS: white with a yellow center, in whorls of 3 on a loosely flowered upright stem, about 1¼" (3.1 cm) wide, with 3 rounded petals. PLANT: aquatic, 4–36" (10–91 cm) tall; leaves basal, erect, simple, arrowhead-shaped, long-stalked, margin entire, green. HABITAT: shallow water. COMMENTS: several other species of *Sagittaria*, some with very narrow leaves, also occur in New York.

LEAVES WHORLED, SIMPLE

White Trillium
• *Trillium grandiflorum* (Michx.) Salisb.
• Lily family **Liliaceae**
FLOWERING SEASON: late April through May. FLOWER: white, becoming pink just before wilting, solitary and terminal on a tall erect stalk, about 3" (7.5 cm) wide, with 3 large, evenly whorled petals; petals ovate with a tapering, pointed tip, often slightly recurved. PLANT: 8–18" (20–45 cm) tall; leaves 3, in a whorl at the base of the flower stalk, simple, ovate with a tapering, pointed tip and an entire margin, practically stalkless, green. HABITAT: woodlands. COMMENTS: the name trillium refers to three, the number of leaves, sepals, and petals. New York's largest flowered trillium.

Painted Trillium
• *Trillium undulatum* Willd.
• Lily family **Liliaceae**
FLOWERING SEASON: May. FLOWER: white with crimson veins around the center, solitary and terminal on an erect stalk; about 2" (5 cm) wide, with 3 evenly whorled petals, petals lance-shaped with a tapering, pointed tip. PLANT: 8–24" (20–60 cm) tall; leaves 3, in a whorl at the base of the flower stalk, simple, ovate with a tapering, pointed tip and an entire margin, short-stalked, green. HABITAT: woodlands.

Nodding Trillium
• *Trillium cernuum* L.
• Lily family **Liliaceae**
FLOWERING SEASON: mid-May to mid-June. FLOWER: white, solitary and terminal on a drooping stalk characteristically oriented below the leaves, with 3 evenly whorled petals, petals about 1" (2.5 cm) long, broadly lance-shaped, deeply recurved. PLANT: 8–20" (20–50 cm) tall; leaves 3, in a whorl at the base of the flower stalk, simple, broadly ovate with a pointed tip and an entire margin, stalkless or nearly so, green. HABITAT: moist woodlands, wooded swamps.

FLOWERS SYMMETRICAL, WITH 4 PETALS OR PETAL-LIKE PARTS

AQUATIC, LEAVES IN A FLOATING ROSETTE

Water-chestnut
• *Trapa natans* L.
• Water-chestnut family **Trapaceae**
FLOWERING SEASON: July into August. FLOWERS: white, one to few, terminal, supported by floating leaves, about ¼" (6 mm) wide, with 4 somewhat unequal rounded petals. PLANT: aquatic, submerged stem 1–4' (0.3–1.2 m) long; submerged leaves opposite, pinnately compound with thread-like segments; floating leaves in a terminal rosette, simple, fan-shaped, long-stemmed, margin sharply toothed, glossy, green. HABITAT: ponds, lakes, and slow-moving water. COMMENTS: a troublesome aquatic weed that produces a hard-shelled fruit with 4 sharp spines *capable of inflicting painful injury.*

Arrowhead, Wapato / *Sagittaria latifolia*

White Trillium / *Trillium grandiflorum*

Painted Trillium / *Trillium undulatum*

Nodding Trillium / *Trillium cernuum*

Water-chestnut / *Trapa natans*

LEAVES ALTERNATE, SIMPLE

Garlic Mustard
•*Alliaria petiolata* (Bieb.) Cav. and Grande
•Mustard family **Brassicaceae**
FLOWERING SEASON: May. FLOWERS:
white, few to several in a terminal cluster,
about $5/16$" (8 mm) wide, cross-shaped,
with 4 narrowly oval petals. PLANT: 1–3'
(30–90 cm) tall; leaves alternate, simple,
heart-shaped to triangular, margin
coarsely toothed, green; seed pods 1–2"
(2.5–5 cm) long, very slender. HABITAT:
roadsides, waste areas, fields, and woodlands. COMMENTS: crushed leaves have
a garlic-like odor.

Wild Peppergrass
•*Lepidium virginicum* L.
•Mustard family **Brassicaceae**
FLOWERING SEASON: mid-May to July.
FLOWERS: white, many in slender terminal clusters, about $1/16$" (1.6 mm) wide,
cross-shaped, with 4 oval petals. PLANT:
6–24" (15–60 cm) tall; leaves alternate
and basal, simple, upper leaves lance-
shaped, margin sharply toothed or
entire, basal leaves obovate with tiny
lobes along the stalk, margin toothed,
green; seed pods about $5/8$" (1.6 cm)
long, nearly round, notched. HABITAT:
fields and roadsides. COMMENTS: field-
cress, *Lepidium campestre*, has oblong
to paddle-shaped basal leaves and narrowly arrowhead-shaped stem leaves.

Sea-rocket
•*Cakile edentula* (Bigel.) Hook.
•Mustard family **Brassicaceae**
FLOWERING SEASON: July–August. FLOW-
ERS: white to pale purple, few in a terminal cluster, about $1/4$" (5 mm) wide,
cross-shaped, with 4 oval petals. PLANT:
8–12" (20–30 cm) tall; leaves alternate,
simple, lance-shaped, margin unevenly
toothed, green; seed pods $1/2$–$3/4$"
(1.3–1.9 cm) long, 2-sectioned, upper
section slightly larger, ovoid. HABITAT:
coastal sandy soil, also along Lake Erie.

Canadian Mayflower
•*Maianthemum canadense* Desf.
•Lily family **Liliaceae**
FLOWERING SEASON: late May to late June.
FLOWERS: white, up to 20 in an oval terminal cluster 1–2" (2.5–5 cm) long, individual flowers about $3/16$" (5 mm) wide,
with 4 oblong petal-like parts. PLANT:
2–7" (5–17.5 cm) tall; leaves usually 2,
alternate, simple, somewhat heart-
shaped, margin entire, green, glossy.
HABITAT: woodlands. COMMENTS: unusu-
al in that most members of the lily family
have perianth parts in multiples of 3.
Also known as the false or wild lily-of-
the-valley.

LEAVES ALTERNATE, COMPOUND
OR DEEPLY DIVIDED

Cut-leaf Toothwort
•*Cardamine concatenata* (Michx.) Schwein
•Mustard family **Brassicaceae**
FLOWERING SEASON: late April to mid-
May. FLOWERS: white, few to several, in a
terminal cluster, about $5/8$" (1.6 cm)
wide, cross-shaped, with 4 oval petals.
PLANT: 8–15" (20–37.5 cm) tall; leaves
alternate, deeply divided, margin coarsely toothed, green; seed pods 1–1$1/2$"
(2.5–3.8 cm) long, slender, spreading.
HABITAT: woodlands. COMMENTS: two-
leaf toothwort, *Cardamine diphylla*,
which blooms just after the cut-leaf
toothwort, has leaves with 3 broad ovate
divisions.

Sea-rocket / *Cakile edentula*

Garlic Mustard / *Alliaria petiolata*

Wild Peppergrass / *Lepidium virginicum*

Cut-leaf Toothwort / *Cardamine concate-nata*

Canadian Mayflower / *Maianthemum canadense*

Watercress

- *Rorippa nasturtium-aquaticum* (L.) Hayek
- Mustard family **Brassicaceae**

FLOWERING SEASON: June into August. FLOWERS: white, several in terminal clusters, about ³⁄₁₆" (5 mm) wide, cross-shaped, with 4 oval petals. PLANT: aquatic; leaves alternate, pinnately compound with 3 to 9 segments, margins uneven, green; seed pods about 1" (2.5 cm) long, slender, long-stalked, spreading. HABITAT: in brooks, streams, and drainage ditches.

LEAVES OPPOSITE OR WHORLED, SIMPLE

Bunchberry

- *Cornus canadensis* L.
- Dogwood family **Cornaceae**

FLOWERING SEASON: June. FLOWERHEAD: white with a greenish center, about 1" (2.5 cm) wide, rimmed by 4 to 6 large white petal-like bracts; individual flowers tiny, greenish, with 4 minute petals. PLANT: 3–9" (7.5–22.5 cm) tall; leaves whorled, simple, ovate with a pointed tip, margin entire, green; fruit a ¼" (6 mm) wide "bunched cluster" of smooth bright red berries. HABITAT: woodlands.

Sweet-scented Bedstraw

- *Galium triflorum* Michx.
- Madder family **Rubiaceae**

FLOWERING SEASON: June–July. FLOWERS: white to greenish white, many in 3-branched terminal and axial clusters, tiny, corolla with 4 sharply pointed, petal-like lobes. PLANT: 1–3' (30–90 cm) tall; leaves whorled in groups of 6 on a smooth stalk, simple, narrowly oval, margin entire, green. HABITAT: fields and waste areas. COMMENTS: goosegrass, *Galium aparine*, has a spiny stem, rough leaves, and small clusters of axial flowers. About 20

Galium species have been reported from this state.

Woodruff

- *Galium odoratum* (L.) Scop.
- Madder family **Rubiaceae**

FLOWERING SEASON: mid-May to mid-June. FLOWERS: white, several, in flat-topped terminal clusters, about ¼" (6 mm) wide, tubular with 4 sharp, petal-like lobes. PLANT: 4–7" (10–17.5 cm) tall; leaves in 3 or 4 whorls of about 8, simple, lance-shaped, margin entire, green. HABITAT: waste areas, meadows, and open woodlands. COMMENTS: this herb is used to flavor May wine.

Partridge-berry, Twin-berry

- *Mitchella repens* L.
- Madder family **Rubiaceae**

FLOWERING SEASON: late June through July. FLOWERS: white, in terminal pairs, up to ½" (1.3 cm) long, tubular with 4 pointed and often recurved, petal-like lobes. PLANT: prostrate; leaves opposite on 6–12" (15–30 cm) long stems, simple, nearly round, margin entire, green, often with whitish veining, evergreen. HABITAT: woodlands. COMMENTS: the bright red berries are edible but bland.

LEAVES OPPOSITE, COMPOUND

Virgin's-bower

- *Clematis virginiana* L.
- Crowfoot family **Ranunculaceae**

FLOWERING SEASON: late July through August. FLOWERS: white, several in showy axial clusters, about 1" (2.5 cm) wide, with 4 narrowly oblong petal-like sepals and numerous prominent thread-like stamens. PLANT: a climbing vine up to 10' (3 m) long; leaves opposite, with 3 lance-shaped occasionally lobed leaflets, margins unevenly toothed, green. HABITAT: open woodlands, hedgerows, and

Bunchberry / *Cornus canadensis*

Sweet-scented Bedstraw / *Galium triflo-rum*

Watercress / *Rorippa nasturtium-aquaticum*

Woodruff / *Galium odoratum*

Virgin's-bower / *Clematis virginiana*

Partridge-berry, Twin-berry / *Mitchella repens*

wooded swamps. COMMENTS: this species produces showy clusters of plumed seeds.

~~

FLOWERS SYMMETRICAL, WITH 5 PETALS OR PETAL-LIKE PARTS

LEAVES BASAL, SIMPLE

Spathulate-leaved Sundew
•*Drosera intermedia* Hayne
•Sundew family **Droseraceae**
FLOWERING SEASON: July into August. FLOWERS: white, several, in a slender terminal cluster, about $1/4$" (6 mm) wide, with 5 oblong petals. PLANT: 3–8" (7.5–20 cm) tall; leaves basal, simple, spoon-shaped with long stalks, upper surface covered with reddish glandular hairs with a sticky, syrup-like coating, margin entire, green. HABITAT: bogs, fens, and wet sand. COMMENTS: a carnivorous plant that uses its sticky hairs to entrap insects. Round-leaved sundew, *Drosera rotundifolia*, has nearly round leaves, while thread-leaved sundew, *D. filiformis* has long, narrow, thread-like leaves.

Round-leaf Pyrola
•*Pyrola americana* Sweet
•Shinleaf family **Pyrolaceae**
FLOWERING SEASON: late June through July. FLOWERS: white, several to many on a spike-like terminal cluster, about $3/4$" (1.9 cm) wide, with 5 rounded petals, nodding. PLANT: 6–20" (15–50 cm) tall; leaves basal, simple, nearly round, margin minutely toothed, green. HABITAT: woodlands.

Bird's-eye Primrose
•*Primula mistassinica* Michx.
•Primrose family **Primulaceae**
FLOWERING SEASON: late May to early June. FLOWERS: pinkish white to pale purple, with or without a yellow eye, 2 to 8 in a long-stalked terminal cluster, about $3/16$" (5 mm) long, tubular with 5 spreading, notched, petal-like lobes. PLANT: 1–6" (2.5–15 cm) tall; leaves basal, simple, paddle-shaped, margin minutely toothed, green. HABITAT: wet rocky areas. COMMENTS: *protected. Threatened. Do not disturb.*

Early Saxifrage
•*Saxifraga virginiensis* Michx.
•Saxifrage family **Saxifragaceae**
FLOWERING SEASON: late April through May. FLOWERS: white, many on a branched terminal cluster, up to $1/4$" (6 mm) wide, with 5 rounded petals. PLANT: 4–12" (10–30 cm) tall; leaves mostly basal, simple, ovate with a bluntly toothed margin, green. HABITAT: rocky, usually moist soils, often on wet cliffs.

Grass-of-Parnassus
•*Parnassia glauca* Raf.
•Saxifrage family **Saxifragaceae**
FLOWERING SEASON: August–September. FLOWER: white with greenish veins, solitary, terminal, about 1" (2.5 cm) wide, with 5 oval petals. PLANT: 8–24" (20–60 cm) tall; leaves mostly basal, with 1 on the stem, simple, broadly egg-shaped to nearly round, margin entire, green. HABITAT: swamps and moist meadows.

Foamflower
•*Tiarella cordifolia* L.
•Saxifrage family **Saxifragaceae**
FLOWERING SEASON: mid-May to mid-June. FLOWERS: white, about a dozen in a narrow terminal cluster, about $1/4$" (6 mm) wide, with 5 narrow petals and 10 long conspicuous stamens that give the flower a feathery appearance. PLANT: 6–12" (15–30 cm) tall; leaves basal, simple, heart-shaped with 3 to 7 angular lobes, margins toothed, green. HABITAT: woodlands.

Early Saxifrage / *Saxifraga virginiensis*

Round-leaf Pyrola / *Pyrola americana*

Bird's-eye Primrose / *Primula mistassinica*

Grass-of-Parnassus / *Parnassia glauca*

Spathulate-leaved Sundew / *Drosera intermedia*

Foamflower / *Tiarella cordifolia*

Dewdrop, False Violet
•*Dalibarda repens* L.
•Rose family **Rosaceae**
FLOWERING SEASON: late July to mid-August. FLOWERS: white, 1 or 2 arising in leaf axils, about $^3/_8$" (9 mm) wide, with 5 rounded petals. PLANT: creeping, 2–6" (5–15 cm) long; leaves basal, simple, heart-shaped, margin scalloped, pubescent on both sides, green. HABITAT: open woodlands and fen borders.

LEAVES BASAL, COMPOUND

Goldthread
•*Coptis trifolia* (L.) Salisb.
•Crowfoot family **Ranunculaceae**
FLOWERING SEASON: May.   FLOWER: white, solitary, terminal, about ½" (1.3 cm) wide, with 5 to 7 lance-shaped, petal-like sepals. PLANT: 3–6" (7.5–15 cm) tall; leaves basal, long-stalked, compound with 3 fan-shaped, sharply toothed leaflets, green, glossy, evergreen. HABITAT: damp woods. COMMENTS: named for its slender yellow-orange roots.

Wild Strawberry
•*Fragaria virginiana* Mill
•Rose family **Rosaceae**
FLOWERING SEASON: May.   FLOWERS: white with a yellow center, few, in a terminal cluster, about $^3/_4$" (1.9 cm) wide, with 5 rounded petals. PLANT: creeping, 3–6" (7.5–15 cm) tall; leaves appearing basal, 3-lobed; leaflets broadly oval to obovate, margins toothed, green; fruit red, ovoid, fragrant, edible. HABITAT: fields and edges of woodlands.

Common Wood-sorrel
•*Oxalis acetosella* L.
•Oxalis family **Oxalidaceae**
FLOWERING SEASON: late May through July. FLOWERS: pinkish white to white with dark pink veins, solitary to several in leaf axils, about $^3/_4$" (1.9 cm) wide, with 5 rounded petals. PLANT: 2–6" (5–15 cm) tall; leaves appearing basal, compound with 3 leaflets; leaflets heart-shaped, margin entire, green. HABITAT: moist woodlands.

LEAVES ALTERNATE, SIMPLE

Poke, Pokeweed
•*Phytolacca americana* L.
•Pokeweed family **Phytolaccaceae**
FLOWERING SEASON: July to early August. FLOWERS: white with a green center, many on slender 2–8" (5–20cm) long, loosely flowered terminal and axial clusters, up to $^1/_4$" (6 mm) wide, with 5 rounded, petal-like divisions. PLANT: 4–12' (1.2–3.6 m) tall; leaves alternate on a purplish stem, large, simple, broadly lance-shaped, margin entire, green; fruit a grape-like cluster of very dark purple inedible berries. HABITAT: meadows and woodlots.

Japanese Knotweed, Japanese Bamboo
•*Polygonum cuspidatum*
 Sieb. and Zucc.
•Buckwheat family **Polygonaceae**
FLOWERING SEASON: mid-August through September. FLOWERS: white, many in slender, 2–4" (5–10 cm) long terminal and upper axial clusters, minute, with 5 petal-like lobes. PLANT: 4–8' (1.2–2.4 m) tall; appearing shrub-like but stems not perennial; leaves alternate on a bamboo-like stem, simple, broadly ovate with a somewhat squared base, margin entire, green. HABITAT: fields, waste areas, roadsides, thickets, and moist soil

Dewdrop, False Violet / *Dalibarda repens*

Goldthread / *Coptis trifolia*

Poke, Pokeweed / *Phytolacca americana*

Wild Strawberry / *Fragaria virginiana*

Common Wood-sorrel / *Oxalis acetosella*

Japanese Knotweed, Japanese Bamboo / *Polygonum cuspidatum*

Cheese Mallow
•*Malva neglecta* Wallr.
•Mallow family **Malvaceae**
FLOWERING SEASON: June–August. FLOW-ERS: whitish with lavender veins, some-times with a bluish tinge, 1 to several, in axils along the stem, about $1/2$" (1.3 cm) wide with 5 broad petals notched at the tip. PLANT: 4–12" (10–30 cm) long, mostly prostrate; leaves alternate, simple, heart-shaped with a rounded tip, shal-lowly lobed, margin scalloped to some-what toothed, green. HABITAT: fields and waste areas. COMMENTS: called cheeses in reference to the wheel-shaped fruit.

Labrador Tea
•*Rhododendron groenlandicum*
 (Oeder) Kron & Judd
•Heath family **Ericaceae**
FLOWERING SEASON: June. FLOWERS: white, several to many in a rounded ter-minal cluster, $1/4$–$3/8$" (6–9 mm) wide, tubular at the base with 5 spreading, petal-like lobes. PLANT: shrub, about 1–3' (30–90 cm) tall; leaves alternate, simple, oblong with an inrolled margin, dark green above, downy and white (young leaves) to rusty (mature leaves) below, evergreen. HABITAT: bogs, fens, swamps, and drier acidic soils. COM-MENTS: specimens growing at higher ele-vations are often stunted.

Trailing Arbutus
•*Epigaea repens* L.
•Heath family **Ericaceae**
FLOWERING SEASON: mid-April to mid-May. FLOWERS: white to pink, several, in a terminal cluster, about $1/2$" (1.3 cm) wide, tubular at the base with 5 spread-ing, petal-like lobes; fragrant. PLANT: prostrate on the ground; leaves alternate along a hairy woody stem, simple, oval with an entire margin, green, evergreen. HABITAT: sandy or rocky woods, especial-ly under evergreens.

Large Cranberry
•*Vaccinium macrocarpon* Ait.
•Heath family **Ericaceae**
FLOWERING SEASON: mid-June through July. FLOWERS: white to pinkish white with a brownish cone-shaped center, many, axial, about $5/16$" (8 mm) wide, tubular with 4 narrow, deeply re-curved, petal-like lobes. PLANT: woody, branched, trailing; leaves alternate, sim-ple, oblong, small, margin entire, green; fruit an acidic, ovoid red berry. HABITAT: bogs, fen meadows.

Mountain Laurel
•*Kalmia latifolia* L.
•Heath family **Ericaceae**
FLOWERING SEASON: mid-June to mid-July. FLOWERS: white to pinkish, many, in a spherical terminal cluster, $3/4$–1" (1.9–2.5 cm) wide, saucer-shaped with 5 shallowly pointed lobes. PLANT: shrub, 5–15' (1.5–4.5 m) tall; leaves alternate, simple, lance-shaped with an entire mar-gin, green, evergreen. HABITAT: in sandy or rocky soil in woodlands. COMMENTS: bees visiting these flowers are said to pro-duce poisonous honey.

Meadow-sweet
•*Spiraea latifolia* (Ait.) Borkh.
•Rose family **Rosaceae**
FLOWERING SEASON: July to mid-August. FLOWERS: white with pinkish centers, many in showy upright, 3–5" (7.5–12.5 cm) terminal and axial clus-ters, about $5/16$" (8 mm) wide, with 5 rounded petals. PLANT: shrub, 2–5' (0.6–1.5 m) tall; leaves alternate, simple, oblong, margin coarsely and unevenly toothed, green. HABITAT: swamps, meadows, and roadsides.

Large Cranberry / *Vaccinium macrocarpon*

Cheese Mallow / *Malva neglecta*

Mountain Laurel / *Kalmia latifolia*

Labrador Tea / *Rhododendron groenlandicum*

Meadow-sweet / *Spiraea latifolia*

Trailing Arbutus / *Epigaea repens*

Black Nightshade
- *Solanum ptycanthum* Dunal
- Nightshade family **Solanaceae**

FLOWERING SEASON: late July to mid-September. FLOWERS: white with a protruding yellow center, few to several, in loose clusters, about $5/16$" (8 mm) wide, corolla with 5 spreading and somewhat recurved, sharply pointed, petal-like lobes. PLANT: $1-2^1/2$' (0.3–0.8 m) tall; leaves alternate, simple, ovate, margin usually entire, green; fruit a black berry. HABITAT: waste areas.

Horse-nettle
- *Solanum carolinense* L.
- Nightshade family **Solanaceae**

FLOWERING SEASON: late June through August. FLOWERS: white to bluish white with a protruding yellow center, several, in a loose terminal cluster, about 1" (2.5 cm) wide, corolla shaped like a 5-pointed star. PLANT: about $1-3$' (30–90 cm) tall; leaves alternate on a spiny stem, simple, ovate with several deeply cleft, sharply pointed lobes, green. HABITAT: roadsides, meadows, cultivated fields, and waste areas.

Jimsonweed
- *Datura stramonium* L.
- Nightshade family **Solanaceae**

FLOWERING SEASON: August–September. FLOWERS: white, sometimes with a purplish center, several, scattered throughout the plant in axils, up to 4" (10 cm) long, corolla bell-shaped with 5 flaring sharp lobes. PLANT: $1-5$' (0.3–1.5 m) tall; leaves alternate, simple, ovate, margin with several large, sharp-tipped lobes, green. HABITAT: fields, pastures, and waste areas, sometimes close to the ocean.

Moth-mullein
- *Verbascum blatteria* L.
- Figwort family **Scrophulariaceae**

FLOWERING SEASON: mid-June through August. FLOWERS: yellow or white, several, in a loose-flowered, slender terminal cluster, about 1" (2.5 cm) wide, tubular at the base with 5 rounded petal-like lobes. PLANT: $2-6$' (0.6–1.8 m) tall; leaves basal and alternate, simple, oblong to lance-shaped with a pointed tip, margin toothed, green. HABITAT: fields and waste areas.

LEAVES ALTERNATE, COMPOUND

Red Raspberry
- *Rubus idaeus* L.
- Rose family **Rosaceae**

FLOWERING SEASON: June. FLOWERS: white, several to many, in loose axial and terminal clusters, about $1/2$" (1.3 cm) wide, with 5 rounded petals. PLANT: shrub, about $3-6$' (0.9–1.8 m) tall; leaves alternate, pinnately compound with 5 leaflets on the lower stem and 3 on the upper stem; leaflets oblong with a pointed tip, margins coarsely and irregularly toothed, green; fruit berry-like, round, bright red, juicy; stem spiny. HABITAT: edges of woodlands, woodland trails, and disturbed soils. COMMENTS: raspberry species have pinnately compound leaves, round stems, and berries that easily separate from their stalks. Blackberry species have palmately compound leaves, angular stems, and berries that are tightly fixed to their stalks.

Dewberry
- *Rubus flagellaris* Willd.
- Rose family **Rosaceae**

FLOWERING SEASON: June. FLOWERS: white, several scattered along the plant, about 1" (2.5 cm) wide, with 5 rounded petals. PLANT: prostrate; leaves alternate on a thorned stem, compound with 3 leaflets; leaflets ovate, margins toothed, green. HABITAT: open woodlands. COMMENTS: the name dewberry is commonly applied to any blackberry or raspberry with a prostrate stem.

Black Nightshade / *Solanum ptycanthum*

Moth-mullein / *Verbascum blatteria*

Red Raspberry / *Rubus idaeus*

Jimsonweed / *Datura stramonium*

Horse-nettle / *Solanum carolinense*

Dewberry / *Rubus flagellaris*

White Avens
• *Geum canadense* Jacq.
• Rose family **Rosaceae**
FLOWERING SEASON: mid-June to mid-July. FLOWERS: white, several in terminal clusters, about ⅝" (1.6 cm) wide, with 5 rounded petals. PLANT: $1\frac{1}{2}$–$2\frac{1}{2}$' (45–75 cm) tall; leaves basal and alternate; basal leaves with 3 lobes or pinnately compound; stem leaves typically with 3 lobes; leaflets broadly ovate or lance-shaped, margins toothed, green; stem hairy. HABITAT: woodlands.

Tall Cinquefoil
• *Potentilla arguta* Pursh
• Rose family **Rosaceae**
FLOWERING SEASON: June–July. FLOWERS: white with a yellow center, few to several in a rounded terminal cluster, about ½" (1.3 cm) wide, with 5 nearly round petals. PLANT: 1-4' (0.3-1.2 m) tall; leaves alternate, pinnately compound with 7 to 11 leaflets; leaflets ovate, margins toothed, green. HABITAT: dry or rocky soil.

Meadow-sweet, Queen-of-the meadow
• *Filipendula ulmaria* (L.) Maxim.
• Rose family **Rosaceae**
FLOWERING SEASON: mid-to late July. FLOWERS: white to off-white, many in a large, showy terminal cluster, about ⅜" (9 mm) wide, with 5 rounded petals; fragrant. PLANT: 2-4' (0.6-1.2 m) tall; leaves alternate, pinnately compound; leaflets ovate to lance-shaped, margins toothed, green. HABITAT: meadows.

False Spiraea
• *Sorbaria sorbifolia* (L.) A. Br.
• Rose family **Rosaceae**
FLOWERING SEASON: late June to mid-July. FLOWERS: white, many, in showy, dense, elongated terminal clusters, about ¼" (6 mm) wide, with 5 nearly round

petals. PLANT: shrub, 3-6' (0.9-1.8 m) tall; leaves alternate, pinnately compound with 11 to 15 leaflets; leaflets lance-shaped, margins toothed, green. HABITAT: escaped from cultivation along roadsides, hedgerows, and drainage ditches.

Cow-parsnip
• *Heracleum maximum* Bartr.
• Carrot family **Apiaceae**
FLOWERING SEASON: June. FLOWERS: white, many, in rounded, flat-topped terminal clusters 6-12" (15-30 cm) wide; individual flowers tiny, with 5 petals. PLANT: 4-8' (1.2-2.4 m) tall; leaves alternate, compound with 3 leaflets; leaflets broadly ovate, often lobed, margins toothed, green, stem green. HABITAT: moist, usually shaded soils.

Giant Hogweed
• *Heracleum mantegazzianum* Sommier & Levier
• Carrot family **Apiaceae**
FLOWERING SEASON: mid-June to mid-July. FLOWERS: white, many, in huge, rounded, flat-topped clusters up to 2½' (75 cm) wide, individual flowers small, with 5 petals. PLANT: 6-14' (1.8-4.2 m) tall; leaves huge, up to 5' (1.5 m) long, alternate, compound with 3 leaflets; leaflets deeply cut into lobes, margins sharply toothed, green; leaf stalks and stem green with purplish blotches. HABITAT: sunny, moist meadows and roadsides. COMMENTS: *contact with this plant, which looks like a large cow-parsnip, causes painful burning blisters in susceptible people.*

Cow-parsnip / *Heracleum maximum*

Giant Hogweed / *Heracleum mantegazzianum*

White Avens / *Geum canadense*

Tall Cinquefoil / *Potentilla arguta*

Meadow-sweet, Queen-of-the-meadow / *Fili-pendula ulmaria*

False Spiraea / *Sorbaria sorbifolia*

Water-hemlock, Spotted Cowbane

•*Cicuta maculata* L.

•Carrot family **Apiaceae**

FLOWERING SEASON: July. FLOWERS: white, many, in rounded, flat-topped terminal clusters 2–4" (5–10 cm) wide; individual flowers tiny, with 5 petals. PLANT: 3–6' (0.9–1.8 m) tall; leaves alternate, pinnately compound; 7 to 17 leaflets, lance-shaped with sharp tips, basal leaflets often deeply cleft, margins coarsely toothed, green; stem green with purplish markings. HABITAT: swamps and low grounds. COMMENTS: *extremely poisonous.* Water-parsnip, *Sium suave*, has narrowly lance-shaped, finely toothed leaflets.

Bulb-bearing Water-hemlock

•*Cicuta bulbifera* L.

•Carrot family **Apiaceae**

FLOWERING SEASON: July–August. FLOWERS: white, many, in small, rounded terminal and axial clusters about 1" (2.5 cm) wide; individual flowers with 5 tiny petals. PLANT: 1–3½' (0.3–1.1 m) tall; leaves alternate, divided into several pinnately compound sections; leaflets very narrow, margins sharply toothed, green; bulblet clusters in leaf axils. HABITAT: swamps, edges of ponds and lakes.

Chervil

•*Anthriscus cerefolium* (L.) Hoffm.

•Carrot family **Apiaceae**

FLOWERING SEASON: mid-May to mid-June. FLOWERS: white, many in rounded, flat-topped terminal and axial clusters about 2½" (6.3 cm) wide; individual flowers tiny, with 5 petals. PLANT: 1½–2½' (45–75 cm) tall; leaves alternate, repeatedly and deeply pinnately divided, triangular, fern-like, margin toothed, green; fruit about ¼" (6 mm) long, slender, smooth, very dark. HABITAT: meadows, roadsides, and occasionally open woodlands. COMMENTS: *this plant can be*

very difficult to distinguish from poison hemlock, Conium maculata. Once established, chervil becomes a locally dominant weed. Sweet cicely, *Osmorhiza longistylis*, a similar native woodland species, has smaller flower clusters, smooth stems, and short sharp spines on the fruit; the closely related *O. claytoni* has pubescent stems. Honewort, *Cryptotaenia canadensis*, another common woodland species, has even smaller flower clusters and leaves divided into only 3 ovate leaflets.

Queen-Anne's Lace, Wild Carrot

•*Daucus carota* L.

•Carrot family **Apiaceae**

FLOWERING SEASON: July to mid-September. FLOWERS: white, often with a single tiny purple flower in the center of each cluster, many, in rounded, flat-topped terminal clusters 2–4" (5–10 cm) wide; individual flowers tiny, with 5 petals. PLANT: about 1–3' (0.3–1 m) tall; leaves alternate, with 1 to 3 deeply cleft, pinnately arranged divisions, fern-like, margins toothed, green. HABITAT: fields and waste areas. COMMENTS: caraway, *Carum carvi*, also found in sunny areas, is only 1–2' (30–60 cm) tall, has flower clusters 1–2½" (2.5–6.3 cm) wide, and narrower leaves.

Virginia Waterleaf

•*Hydrophyllum virginianum* L.

•Waterleaf family **Hydrophyllaceae**

FLOWERING SEASON: June. FLOWERS: white to violet, several, in a small, rounded cluster, about $5/16$" (8 mm) long, tubular with 5 oblong, petal-like lobes. PLANT: 1–2' (30–60 cm) tall; leaves alternate, pinnately lobed into 5 to 7 sharply toothed segments, green, often with whitish mottling. HABITAT: woodlands. COMMENTS: broad-leaved waterleaf, *Hydrophyllum canadense*, has similar flowers but broad maple-like leaves.

Bulb-bearing Water-hemlock / *Cicuta bulbifera*

Water-hemlock, Spotted Cowbane / *Cicuta maculata*

Queen-Anne's Lace, Wild Carrot / *Daucus carota*

Virginia Waterleaf / *Hydrophyllum virginianum*

Chervil / *Anthriscus cerefolium*

Yarrow
•*Achillea millefolium* L.
•Aster family **Asteraceae**
FLOWERING SEASON: mid-June to early September. FLOWERS: white, sometimes pinkish, flowerheads many in a rounded, flat-topped terminal cluster, about ¼" (6 mm) wide, rimmed with 4 to 6 petal-like rays. PLANT: 1–2' (30–61 cm) tall; leaves basal and alternate, finely dissected into pinnatified segments, lance-shaped, green. HABITAT: fields, roadsides, and waste areas.

LEAVES OPPOSITE OR WHORLED, SIMPLE

Carolina Spring Beauty
•*Claytonia caroliniana* Michx.
•Purslane family **Portulacaceae**
FLOWERING SEASON: mid-April to mid-May. FLOWERS: white to pinkish with darker pink veins, few, in a loose terminal cluster, about ¾" (1.9 cm) wide, with 5 rounded petals. PLANT: 2–4" (5–10 cm) tall; leaves basal or opposite, simple, broadly lance-shaped, margin entire, green. HABITAT: woodlands. COMMENTS: Spring beauty, *Claytonia virginica*, has much narrower leaves.

Bouncing-bet, Soapwort
•*Saponaria officinalis* L.
•Pink family **Caryophyllaceae**
FLOWERING SEASON: mid-July to early September. FLOWERS: white to pinkish white, many in a dense, rounded terminal cluster, about 1" (2.5 cm) wide, with 5 broad, slightly notched petals. PLANT: 1–2' (30–60 cm) tall; leaves opposite, simple, ovate with a pointed tip, margin entire, green. HABITAT: roadsides, fields, and waste areas.

Mouse-ear Chickweed
•*Cerastium fontanum*
 Baumg. *emend* Jalas.
•Pink family **Caryophyllaceae**
FLOWERING SEASON: May into September. FLOWERS: white, several, in loose terminal clusters, about ¼" (6 mm) wide, with 5 petals deeply cleft nearly to the base. PLANT: spreading, 4–12" (10–30 cm) tall; leaves opposite and basal, oblong, hairy, margin entire, green. HABITAT: fields, meadows, and lawns. COMMENTS: common chickweed, *Stellaria media*, has broader, hairless leaves.

White Campion
•*Silene latifolia* Poir.
•Pink family **Caryophyllaceae**
FLOWERING SEASON: June to early August. FLOWERS: white to pinkish white, few in a loose terminal cluster, about ¾" (1.9 cm) wide, with 5 notched petals and an inflated, hairy, bladder-like base. PLANT: 1–2' (30–60 cm) tall; leaves opposite, simple, broadly lance-shaped, margin entire, green. HABITAT: fields and waste areas.

Sweet Pepper-bush
•*Clethra alnifolia* L.
•White Alder family **Clethraceae**
FLOWERING SEASON: July–August. FLOWERS: white, many, in numerous slender terminal clusters, about ⅜" (9 mm) wide, with 5 rounded petals; spicy fragrance. PLANT: 3–10' (0.9–3 m) tall; leaves alternate on woody branches, simple, obovate, margin sharply toothed, green. HABITAT: swamps and moist woodlands, mostly near the coast.

Yarrow / *Achillea millefolium*

Sweet Pepper-bush / *Clethra alnifolia*

Bouncing-Bet, Soapwort / *Saponaria officinalis*

Mouse-ear Chickweed / *Cerastium fontanum*

White Campion / *Silene latifolia*

Carolina Spring Beauty / *Claytonia caroliniana*

Pipsissewa, Prince's Pine

•*Chimaphila umbellata* (L.) Bart.
•Shinleaf family **Pyrolaceae**
FLOWERING SEASON: mid-to late July.
FLOWERS: white to pinkish white, few to several in a loose terminal cluster, about ½" (1.3 cm) wide, with 5 rounded petals. PLANT: 4–10" (10–25 cm) tall; leaves opposite or whorled, simple, broadly lance-shaped, margin toothed, glossy, green, evergreen. HABITAT: woodlands.

Spotted Wintergreen

•*Chimaphila maculata* (L.) Pursh
•Shinleaf family **Pyrolaceae**
FLOWERING SEASON: July. FLOWERS: white to pinkish, few in a small terminal cluster, about ¾" (1.9 cm) wide, with 5 rounded petals. PLANT: 3–10" (7.5–25 cm) tall; leaves opposite to whorled, simple, lance-shaped, margin sharply toothed, dark green with white central veins. HABITAT: woodlands.

Miterwort

•*Mitella diphylla* L.
•Saxifrage family **Saxifragaceae**
FLOWERING SEASON: May. FLOWERS: white, many on an erect 6–8" (15–20 cm) tall, wand-like cluster, about ⅛" (3 mm) wide, with 5 feathery petals. PLANT: 10–18" (25–45 cm) tall; leaves of 2 types, basal leaves heart-shaped and long-stalked, and a pair of opposite, somewhat lance-shaped leaves about one-third of the way up the stem, margins toothed, green. HABITAT: rich woodlands.

Four-leaf Milkweed

•*Asclepias quadrifolia* Jacq.
•Milkweed family **Asclepiadaceae**
FLOWERING SEASON: June. FLOWERS: white to pinkish white, many, in rounded terminal clusters, about ¼" (6 mm) wide, with 5 deeply recurved petals and a 5-pointed crown-like center. PLANT: 1–2' (30–60 cm) tall; leaves whorled in groups of 4, simple, lance-shaped, margin entire, green. HABITAT: woodlands.

LEAVES OPPOSITE OR WHORLED, COMPOUND

Canada Anemone, Windflower

•*Anemone canadensis* L.
•Crowfoot family **Ranunculaceae**
FLOWERING SEASON: late May to early July. FLOWERS: white, usually 1 to 3, terminal, about 1¼" (3.1 cm) wide, with 5 large, oblong, petal-like sepals. PLANT: 1–2' (30–60 cm) tall; leaves of 2 types, basal leaves long-stalked and 5-lobed, leaves along upper stem whorled or paired, stalkless and 3-lobed, margins sharply and deeply toothed, green; seedhead rounded. HABITAT: low, moist meadows. COMMENTS: long-headed thimbleweed, *Anemone cylindrica*, has upper leaves with lobes divided to their base and a long, cylindrical seedhead.

Dwarf Ginseng

•*Panax trifolius* L.
•Ginseng family **Araliaceae**
FLOWERING SEASON: early to mid-May. FLOWERS: white, several in a small, circular terminal cluster, about 1⁄16" (1.6 mm) wide, with 5 petals and 5 prominent stamens. PLANT: 3–8" (7.5–20 cm) tall; leaves 3, whorled about the stem, palmately compound, with 3 to 5 leaflets; leaflets narrowly lance-shaped, margins toothed, green. HABITAT: woodlands.

Pipsissewa, Prince's Pine / *Chimaphila umbellata*

Spotted Wintergreen / *Chimaphila maculata*

Miterwort / *Mitella diphylla*

Four-leaf Milkweed / *Asclepias quadrifolia*

Dwarf Ginseng / *Panax trifolius*

Canada Anemone, Windflower / *Anemone canadensis*

FLOWERS SYMMETRICAL, WITH 6 PETALS OR PETAL-LIKE PARTS

LEAVES BASAL, SIMPLE

Flowering Rush

•*Butomus umbellatus* L.

•Flowering Rush family **Butomaceae**

FLOWERING SEASON: August. **FLOWERS:** pinkish white to rose with a reddish center, few to several in a flat-topped terminal cluster, about ¾" (1.9 cm) wide, perianth with 3 large, oblong, petal-like parts alternating with 3 short, sharp-tipped, petal-like parts. **PLANT:** 1–4' (0.3–1.2 m) tall; leaves basal, simple, long and very narrow, somewhat triangular in cross section, margin entire, green. **HABITAT:** shorelines of rivers and lakes.

Wild Leek, Ramp

•*Allium tricoccum*

•Lily family **Liliaceae**

FLOWERING SEASON: July. **FLOWERS:** white, many in a nearly spherical terminal cluster on a thin leafless stalk, about ¼" (6 mm) long, perianth with 6 nonspreading parts that give the flower a somewhat tubular appearance. **PLANT:** 1–2' (30–60 cm) tall; leaves usually 2, basal, simple, oblong to lance-shaped, emerging early but withering and disappearing well before flowering, green. **HABITAT:** woodlands. **COMMENTS:** both the leaves and the bulbs are eagerly sought for their powerful garlic-like flavor.

Wild Garlic

•*Allium canadense*

•Lily family **Liliaceae**

FLOWERING SEASON: June. **FLOWERS:** white to pinkish-white, 1 to 3 or more in a terminal cluster with usually 3 sheathing papery bracts beneath, about ¼" (6 mm) wide, perianth with 6 widely spreading, lance-shaped, petal-like parts. **PLANT:** about 1' (30 cm) tall; leaves basal or nearly so, very long and narrow, slightly flattened, green. **HABITAT:** fields, moist meadows. **COMMENTS:** field garlic, *Allium vineale*, is a similar naturalized species with hollow leaves and a single papery bract beneath the flower cluster. Individual flowers have a distinct violet to purplish tinge and a nonspreading perianth, giving the flowers a somewhat tubular appearance.

Nodding Onion

•*Allium cernuum*

•Lily family **Liliaceae**

FLOWERING SEASON: August. **FLOWERS:** white, sometimes with rose to pale purplish tinges, many on a sparsely flowered terminal cluster, about ¼" (6 mm) long; perianth with 6 nonspreading parts that give the flower a tubular appearance. **PLANT:** 1–2½' (30–75 cm) tall; leaves basal, very long and narrow, somewhat flattened, green. **HABITAT:** moist and rocky banks, hillsides, cliffs. **COMMENTS:** *protected. Threatened. Do not disturb.* In New York the range seems to be limited to the south-central Finger Lakes region.

False Asphodel, Sticky Tofieldia

•*Tofieldia glutinosa*

•Lily family **Liliaceae**

FLOWERING SEASON: mid-June to early July. **FLOWERS:** white, many in an oblong terminal cluster, about ¼" (6 mm) wide, perianth with 6 narrow, petal-like parts. **PLANT:** 6–20" (15–50 cm) tall; leaves 2 to 4, basal, simple, long and narrow, flattened, margin entire, green. **HABITAT:** bogs and along rivers. **COMMENTS:** *protected. Endangered. Do not disturb.* The alternate common name sticky tofieldia refers to the adhesive stem.

Flowering Rush / *Butomus umbellatus*

Wild Garlic / *Allium canadense*

Nodding Onion / *Allium cernuum*

False Asphodel, Sticky Tofielda / *Tofieldia glutinosa*

Wild Leek, Ramp / *Allium tricoccum*

Yucca

- *Yucca filamentosa* L.
- Agave family **Agavaceae**

FLOWERING SEASON: July–August. **FLOWERS:** white, many on a showy branching terminal cluster, about 2" (5 cm) long, perianth with 6 ovate petal-like parts, nodding. **PLANT:** 2–10' (0.6–3 m) tall; leaves basal, simple, long and narrow, stiff and sharp-tipped, margin entire with curly hair-like filaments, green. **HABITAT:** sandy soils. **COMMENTS:** although it is a coastal species, on occasion it has escaped cultivation further inland. It is common to find a single powder blue yucca moth in each flower.

LEAVES ALTERNATE, SIMPLE

False Solomon's Seal

Maianthemum racemosa L.

Lily family **Liliaceae**

FLOWERING SEASON: late May to mid-June. **FLOWERS:** white to off-white, many in a branched terminal cluster 1–4" (2.5–10 cm) long, individual flowers about $3/16$" (5 mm) wide, perianth with 6 oblong petal-like parts. **PLANT:** 1–3' (30–90 cm) long; leaves alternate, simple, broadly lance-shaped, margin entire, green; fruit a finely speckled pinkish berry. **HABITAT:** woodlands.

Starry False Solomon's Seal

- *Maianthemum stellata* L.
- Lily family **Liliaceae**

FLOWERING SEASON: mid-May to mid-June. **FLOWERS:** white, several in a short but showy terminal cluster, about ½" (7 mm) wide; perianth with 6 long, narrow, petal-like parts. **PLANT:** 8–20" (20–50 cm) tall; leaves alternate, simple, lance-shaped with bases somewhat clasping the stem, margin entire, green; fruit a greenish berry with 6 black stripes. **HABITAT:** moist woodlands, swamps.

Three-leaved Solomon's Seal

- *Maianthemum trifolia* L.
- Lily family **Liliaceae**

FLOWERING SEASON: June. **FLOWERS:** white, several in a terminal cluster, about $3/8$" (9 mm) wide, perianth with 6 lance-shaped, petal-like parts. **PLANT:** 2–15" (5–37.5 cm) tall; leaves usually 3, alternate, simple, lance-shaped with base somewhat clasping the stem, margin entire, green; fruit a red berry. **HABITAT:** bogs, fens, moist woodlands.

White Mandarin

- *Streptopus amplexifolius* (L.) DC.
- Lily family **Liliaceae**

FLOWERING SEASON: June. **FLOWERS:** greenish white, several, found singly or occasionally two in axils, about ½" (1.3 cm) long, bell-shaped with 6 sharply pointed deeply recurved tips, pendant. **PLANT:** 1½–3' (45–90 cm) tall; leaves alternate along an angularly twisted stalk, simple, broadly lance-shaped with a rounded base that clasps the stem, margin entire, green. **HABITAT:** moist woodlands and wooded swamps.

Wild Cucumber, Wild Balsam-apple, Prickly Cucumber

- *Echinocystis lobata* (Michx.) Tour. and Gray
- Gourd family **Cucurbitaceae**

FLOWERING SEASON: August to early September. **FLOWERS:** white, many, in erect, slender axial clusters, about $5/8$" (1.6 cm) wide, with 6 very narrow petal-like lobes. **PLANT:** climbing vine, 15–25' (4.5–7.5 m) long; leaves alternate, simple, maple-like with 3 to 7 lobes; margin minutely toothed, green; fruit about 2" (5 cm) long, ovoid, coated with slender flexible spines. **HABITAT:** riverbanks, hedgerows, and waste areas.

Wild Cucumber, Wild Balsam-apple, Prickly
Cucumber / *Echinocystis lobata*

Three-leaved Solomon's Seal / *Maianthemum
trifolia*

False Solomon's Seal / *Maianthemum racemosa*

Starry False Solomon's Seal / *Maianthemum
stellata*

Yucca / *Yucca filamentosa*

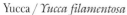

White Mandarin / *Streptopus amplexifolius*

LEAVES OPPOSITE, DEEPLY LOBED

May-apple
• *Podophyllum peltatum* L.
• Barberry family **Berberidaceae**
FLOWERING SEASON: mid-May to mid-June. FLOWERS: white, solitary, axial, about 2" (5 cm) wide, with usually 6 broad, petal-like sepals and 6 to 9 tiny oblong petals in the center. PLANT: 1–1½' (30–45 cm) tall; leaves 2 on flowering plants, opposite, appearing terminal, deeply cleft into 5 to 7 lobes, margin toothed, green. HABITAT: woodlands.

FLOWERS SYMMETRICAL, WITH 7 OR MORE PETALS OR PETAL-LIKE PARTS

AQUATIC, LEAVES FLOATING

White Water-lily, Fragrant Water-lily
• *Nymphaea odorata* Dryand. ex Ait.
• Waterlily family **Nymphaeaceae**
FLOWERING SEASON: mid-June to mid-August. FLOWERS: white, solitary, terminal, 3–5½" (7.5–13.8 cm) wide, with numerous narrowly oblong petals; fragrant. PLANT: leaves up to 1' (30 cm) long, floating, nearly round with a deeply cleft base, margin entire, green on upper surface, purplish below. HABITAT: aquatic (ponds, lakes, and slowly moving streams).

LEAVES BASAL, SIMPLE

English Daisy, Lawn Daisy
• *Bellis perennis* L.
• Aster family **Asteraceae**
FLOWERING SEASON: April–May. FLOWERS: white to pinkish white with a yellow center, flowerheads solitary to several, terminal, ½–1" (1.3–2.5 cm) wide, rimmed with numerous petal-like rays. PLANT: 1–8" (2.5–20 cm) tall; leaves basal, simple, obovate, margin slightly toothed, green. HABITAT: lawns and waste areas.

LEAVES BASAL, LOBED OR DEEPLY DIVIDED

Bloodroot
• *Sanguinaria canadensis* L.
• Poppy family **Papaveraceae**
FLOWERING SEASON: April. FLOWERS: white, solitary, terminal, about 1¼" (3.1 cm) wide, with 8 to 12 oblong petals. PLANT: 6–14" (15–35 cm) tall; leaves basal, palmate, with 5 to 9 lobes, margin uneven, green. HABITAT: woodlands. COMMENTS: the damaged root exudes reddish sap.

Hepatica
• *Hepatica nobilis* Mill.
• Crowfoot family **Ranunculaceae**
FLOWERING SEASON: April–May. FLOWERS: pinkish, white or pale blue, several, on individual hairy basal stalks, about ¾" (1.9 cm) wide, with 6 to 12 lance-shaped, petal-like sepals. PLANT: 4–6" (10–15 cm) tall; leaves basal with long hairy stalks, simple, 3-lobed, usually with an entire margin, green mottled with purple, evergreen. HABITAT: woodlands. COMMENTS: both sharp-lobed and blunt-lobed varieties occur in New York.

Twin-leaf
• *Jeffersonia diphylla* (L.) Pers.
• Barberry family **Berberidaceae**
FLOWERING SEASON: mid-April to mid-May. FLOWERS: white, solitary, terminal, about 1" (2.5 cm) wide, with 8 oblong petals. PLANT: 6–8" (15–20 cm) tall when in flower; leaves basal, long-stalked, deeply divided into 2 ovate parts, margin slightly uneven, green. HABITAT: woodlands.

May-apple / *Podophyllum peltatum*

Twin-leaf / *Jeffersonia diphylla*

Bloodroot / *Sanguinaria canadensis*

White Water-lily, Fragrant Water-lily / *Nymphaea odorata*

English Daisy, Lawn Daisy / *Bellis perennis*

Hepatica / *Hepatica nobilis*

LEAVES ALTERNATE, SIMPLE

Ox-eye Daisy
•*Leucanthemum vulgare* Lam.
•Aster family **Asteraceae**
FLOWERING SEASON: late May to late July.
FLOWERS: white with a yellow disc-shaped center; flowerheads few or solitary, terminal, 1–2" (2.5–5 cm) wide, rimmed with 20 to 30 narrow, slightly 2–3 toothed, petal-like rays. PLANT: 1–3' (30–90 cm) tall; leaves alternate, simple, somewhat oblong, margins coarsely and unevenly toothed, green. HABITAT: fields and meadows.

Tall White Aster
•*Aster lanceolatus* Willd.
•Aster family **Asteraceae**
FLOWERING SEASON: September. FLOWERS: white with a yellow center, flowerheads many, terminal and upper axial, about ¾" (1.9 cm) wide, rimmed with about 20 petal-like rays. PLANT: 2–8' (0.6–2.4 m) tall; leaves alternate, simple, lance-shaped, margin toothed, green. HABITAT: moist soil.

Flat-topped White Aster
•*Aster umbellatus* Mill.
•Aster family **Asteraceae**
FLOWERING SEASON: August–September. FLOWERS: white with a yellow center, flowerheads many in a terminal flat-topped cluster, about ¾" (1.9 cm) wide, rimmed with 10 to 15 petal-like rays. PLANT: 2–8' (0.6–2.4 m) tall; leaves alternate, simple, lance-shaped, margin entire, green. HABITAT: moist soil.

White Lettuce, Rattlesnake-root
•*Prenanthes altissima* L.
•Aster family **Asteraceae**
FLOWERING SEASON: late August through September. FLOWERS: greenish to yellowish white; flowerheads several to many, 5 to 7 in terminal and axial clusters, cylindrical, about ½" (1.3 cm) long, with slightly flaring, narrow, petal-like rays tipped with 5 minute teeth, nodding. PLANT: 1–7' (0.3–2.1 m) tall; leaves basal and alternate, simple; basal leaves broad and 5-lobed; alternate leaves lance-shaped and 3-lobed, margin toothed, green. HABITAT: woodlands.

LEAVES ALTERNATE, DEEPLY DIVIDED OR LOBED

Mayweed, Stinkweed, Dog-fennel
•*Anthemis cotula* L.
•Aster family **Asteraceae**
FLOWERING SEASON: July into September. FLOWERS: white with a yellow center, flowerheads several to many in the upper leaf axils, about 1" (2.5 cm) wide, rimmed with 10 to 18 minutely 3-toothed, petal-like rays. PLANT: 1–2' (30–61 cm) tall; leaves alternate, simple, deeply cleft into numerous narrow pinnately arranged lobes, green, unpleasantly fragrant if torn. HABITAT: fields, roadsides, and waste areas.

LEAVES WHORLED, SIMPLE

Starflower
•*Trientalis borealis* Raf.
•Primrose family **Primulaceae**
FLOWERING SEASON: mid-May to late June. FLOWERS: white, 1 to 4, terminal, up to ½" (1.3 cm) wide, with usually 7 petal-like lobes. PLANT: 3–9" (7.5–22.5 cm) tall; leaves in a single whorled cluster, simple, lance-shaped, margin minutely toothed, green. HABITAT: woodlands.

White Lettuce, Rattlesnake-root /
Prenanthes altissima

Ox-eye Daisy / *Leucanthemum vulgare*

Tall White Aster / *Aster lanceolatus*

Starflower / *Trientalis borealis*

Flat-topped White Aster / *Aster umbellatus*

Mayweed, Stinkweed, Dog-fennel / *Anthemis cotula*

LEAVES WHORLED AND BASAL, COMPOUND

Rue Anemone

•*Anemonella thalictrioides* (L.) Spach
•Crowfoot family **Ranunculaceae**
FLOWERING SEASON: late April to mid-May. FLOWERS: white or occasionally pinkish, 3 or more, terminal, about ¾" (2 cm) wide, with 5–10 oval petal-like sepals. PLANT: 4–9" (10–22.5 cm) tall; leaves both basal and whorled below flowers, compound; leaflets long-stalked and shallowly 3-lobed, green. HABITAT: woodlands.

~

FLOWERS NOT RADIALLY SYM-METRICAL; FLOWERS MINUTE, FILAMENTOUS, TUBULAR WITH NO PETAL-LIKE LOBES, OR WITH NO OBVIOUS PETAL-LIKE PARTS

LEAVES LACKING

Indian Pipe

•*Monotropa uniflora* L.
•Indian-pipe family **Monotropaceae**
FLOWERING SEASON: July–August. FLOW-ERS: white to pinkish, solitary, terminal, about ¾" (1.9 cm) long, urn-shaped, with 4–6 petals, nodding. PLANT: 4–10" (10–25 cm) tall; leaves absent; stalk with numerous, tiny leaf-like bracts, white to pinkish, darkening in age. HABITAT: woodlands. COMMENTS: although the urn-shaped flowers appear tubular at first glance, close examination reveals sym-metrical floral parts.

LEAVES BASAL, SIMPLE

Sweet White Violet

•*Viola macloskeyi* Lloyd
•Violet family **Violaceae**
FLOWERING SEASON: April–May. FLOW-ERS: white, sometimes with fine purple veining, several, on individual stalks; up to ½" (1.3 cm) wide, with 5 un-equal, rounded petals. PLANT: 1–6" (2.5–15 cm) tall; leaves basal, simple, ovate to nearly round with a heart-shaped base, margin finely toothed, green. HABITAT: moist woodlands.

Narrow-leaf Plantain, English Plantain

•*Plantago lanceolata* L.
•Plantain family **Plantaginaceae**
FLOWERING SEASON: late May into July. FLOWERS: white, many in a short, ovoid terminal cluster; minute with prominent white-tipped stamens. PLANT: 8–20" (20–50 cm) tall; leaves basal, simple, nar-rowly lance-shaped, margin entire, green. HABITAT: fields, lawns and waste areas. COMMENTS: common plantain, *Plantago major*, has broadly ovate leaves and 2–10" (5–25 cm) long, very slender flower clusters.

Butter-bur

•*Petasites hybridis* (L.) Gaertn., Meyer & Scherb.
•Aster family **Asteraceae**
FLOWERING SEASON: mid-April to early May. FLOWERS: white to pink-purple; flowerheads many in a terminal cylindri-cal cluster on a 6–15" (15–37.5 cm) tall stem, about ½" (1.3 cm) wide, comprised of many filamentous parts. LEAVES: basal, simple, nearly round, margin toothed, just emerging at flowering, 12–24" (30–60 cm) or more wide at maturity, green, pubescent underneath. HABITAT: escaped from cultivation into moist woodlands and waste areas. COMMENTS: sweet coltsfoot, *Petasites frigidus*, is a native species whose leaves are often deeply cleft into 7 to 11 large lobes.

Narrow-leaf Plantain, English Plantain / *Plantago lanceolata*

Butter-bur / *Petasites hybridis*

Rue Anemone / *Anemonella thalictrioides*

Indian Pipe / *Monotropa uniflora*

Sweet White Violet / *Viola macloskeyi*

Pussy's-toes
•*Antennaria neglecta* Green
•Aster family **Asteraceae**
FLOWERING SEASON: May. FLOWERS:
white, flowerheads several in a cluster in
the upper leaf axils, about ¼" (6 mm)
wide. PLANT: up to 1' (30 cm) tall; leaves
alternate and basal, simple, oblanceolate
to narrowly lance-shaped, white, tomentose on the underside, basal leaves with 1
prominent vein, margin entire, green.
HABITAT: fields and roadsides. COM-
MENTS : everlasting, *Antennaria plan-
taginifolia*, has broader basal leaves with
3 prominent veins.

Wild Calla
•*Calla palustris* L.
•Arum family **Araceae**
FLOWERING SEASON: mid-May to early
June. FLOWERS: greenish white, minute,
many on a 1" (2.5 cm) long cylindrical
spike framed by a 1–2½" (2.5–6.3 cm)
long, broadly lance-shaped, pure
white, petal-like spathe. PLANT: 5–10"
(12.5–25 cm) tall; leaves basal, simple,
broadly heart-shaped with long stalks,
margin entire, green. HABITAT: wooded
swamps and moist meadows, often in
standing water.

Rattlesnake Plantain
•*Goodyera tesselata* Lodd.
•Orchid family **Orchidaceae**
FLOWERING SEASON: August. FLOWERS:
white, 15 to 30 on a slender usually 1-
sided terminal cluster, about ¼" (6 mm)
tall and wide, appearing somewhat
spherical, with 6 petal-like parts. PLANT:
usually 5–10" (13–25 cm) tall; leaves
basal, simple, broadly lance-shaped, margin entire, pale bluish green with wide
greenish white net-like reticulation.
HABITAT: damp to dry woodlands. COM-
MENTS: downy rattlesnake plantain,
Goodyera pubescens, has a cylindrical
flower cluster and bluish green leaves

with beautiful fine whitish reticulations.

LEAVES BASAL, COMPOUND OR DEEPLY LOBED

White Clover
•*Trifolium repens* L.
•Bean family **Fabaceae**
FLOWERING SEASON: June to September.
FLOWERS: off-white, sometimes with a
pale pinkish tinge, many, in ¾" (1.9 cm)
tall ovoid flowerheads; individual flowers
about ¼" (6 mm) long, narrow. PLANT:
trailing, 4–12" (10–30 cm) long; leaves
alternate but appearing basal, compound
with 3 leaflets; leaflets obovate, margins
finely toothed, green with a pale green
chevron. HABITAT: fields, lawns, and
waste areas.

Squirrel-corn
•*Dicentra canadensis* (Goldie) Walp.
•Fumitory family **Fumariaceae**
FLOWERING SEASON: late April to mid-
May. FLOWERS: white to greenish white
with a pinkish tint, 4 to 8 in a slender terminal cluster, up to ¾" (1.9 cm) long,
heart-shaped and open near the tip,
nodding. PLANT: 6–12" (15–30 cm) tall;
leaves basal, compound with many long,
narrow divisions, green. HABITAT: woodlands.

Dutchman's-breeches
•*Dicentra cucullaria* (L.) Bernh.
•Fumitory family **Fumariaceae**
FLOWERING SEASON: mid-April to mid-
May. FLOWERS: white, golden yellow
near the tip, several in a slender terminal
cluster, about ¾" (1.9 cm) long, V-
shaped and open near the tip, nodding.
PLANT: 5–10" (12.5–25 cm) tall; leaves
basal, compound with many long, narrow
divisions, green. HABITAT: woodlands.

Pussy's-toes / *Antennaria neglecta*

Squirrel-corn / *Dicentra canadensis*

Rattlesnake Plantain / *Goodyera tesselata*

Wild Calla / *Calla palustris*

Dutchman's-breeches / *Dicentra cucullaria*

White Clover / *Trifolium repens*

LEAVES ALTERNATE, SIMPLE

Lizard's-tail
- *Saururus cernuus* L.
- Lizard's-tail family **Saururaceae**

FLOWERING SEASON: late July through August. FLOWERS: white, many, in slender 4–6" (10–15 cm) long axial clusters; clusters erect with a drooping tip, with usually 6 thread-like stamens and no petal-like parts. PLANT: 2–5' (0.6–1.5 m) tall; leaves alternate, simple, heart-shaped, margin entire, green. HABITAT: swamps and shallow, usually semishaded, water.

Golden-seal
- *Hydrastis canadensis* L.
- Crowfoot family **Ranunculaceae**

FLOWERING SEASON: May. FLOWER: greenish white, solitary, terminal, about ⅜" (9 mm) wide, composed of a rounded cluster of thread-like stamens. PLANT: about 1' (30 cm) tall; leaves 3, 1 basal and 2 alternate on the stem, maple-like with 5 to 9 lobes, margin sharply and unequally toothed, green. HABITAT: woodlands. COMMENTS: *protected. Threatened. Do not disturb.*

Canada Violet
- *Viola canadensis* L.
- Violet family **Violaceae**

FLOWERING SEASON: May–June. FLOWERS: pale violet to nearly white with a yellow center surrounded by fine purple veining, outer surface purple-tinged, several on individual stalks; about ¾" (1.9 cm) wide, with 5 unequal, rounded petals. PLANT: 3–14" (7.5–35 cm) tall; leaves basal and alternate, simple, somewhat heart-shaped, margin toothed, green. HABITAT: woodlands.

Velvet-leaf Blueberry
- *Vaccinium myrtilloides* Michx.
- Heath family **Ericaceae**

FLOWERING SEASON: June. FLOWERS: white, many, in small terminal clusters, nearly ¼" (6 mm) long, waxy, tubular with 5 tiny teeth, nodding. PLANT: shrub, 6–24" (15–60 cm) tall; leaves alternate, simple, oblong with a pointed tip, margin entire, lower surface pubescent, green. HABITAT: moist soils such as fens and swamps.

Wintergreen
- *Gaultheria procumbens* L.
- Heath family **Ericaceae**

FLOWERING SEASON: July to early August. FLOWERS: waxy white, usually 1 to 3, about ¼" (6 mm) long, urn-shaped, somewhat constricted near the tip with 5 slightly flaring teeth, nodding. PLANT: 2–6" (5–15 cm) tall; leaves alternate, clustered near the top of a woody stem, simple, oval with an obscurely toothed margin, green, glossy, evergreen. HABITAT: woodlands, especially under evergreens. COMMENTS: leaves, pleasantly aromatic when torn, are often used to make a delicious solar tea. The fruit, a bright red berry, is also edible.

Bog Rosemary
- *Andromeda glaucophylla* Link
- Heath family **Ericaceae**

FLOWERING SEASON: mid-May to mid-June. FLOWERS: waxy white or pinkish, 3 to 8 in a drooping terminal cluster; ¼" (6 mm) long, urn-shaped, constricted near the tip, with 5 slightly flaring teeth. PLANT: shrub, 3–18" (7.5–45 cm) tall; leaves alternate, simple, narrowly lance-shaped with an entire margin, dark green above, downy and white below, evergreen. HABITAT: bogs and fens. COMMENTS: *reportedly poisonous and not to be confused with culinary rosemary, a member of the mint family.*

Lizard's-tail / *Saururus cernuus*

Golden-seal / *Hydrastis canadensis*

Canada Violet / *Viola canadensis*

Velvet-leaf Blueberry / *Vaccinium myrtilloides*

Wintergreen / *Gaultheria procumbens*

Bog Rosemary / *Andromeda glaucophylla*

Cassandra, Leatherleaf
• *Chamaedaphne calyculata* (L.) Moench
• Heath family **Ericaceae**
FLOWERING SEASON: mid-April to mid-May. FLOWERS: white, several to many in an extended, 1-sided terminal cluster; about ¼" (6 mm) long, tubular with 5 minute teeth, nodding. PLANT: shrub, 2–4' (0.6–1.2 m) tall; leaves alternate, simple, lance-shaped with an obscurely toothed margin, green, evergreen. HABITAT: bogs, fens and swamps. COMMENTS: the alternate common name leatherleaf refers to the texture of the leaves.

Seneca Snakeroot
• *Polygala senega* L.
• Milkweed family **Polygalaceae**
FLOWERING SEASON: mid-May through June. FLOWERS: white or tinged green, many in a slender 1–2" (2.5–5 cm) long, terminal cluster; individual flowers about ⅛" (3 mm) long, rounded. PLANT: 6–12" (15–30 cm) tall; leaves alternate, simple, lance-shaped, margin minutely toothed, green. HABITAT: open woodlands.

Field Bindweed
• *Convolvulus arvensis* L.
• Morning Glory family **Convolvulaceae**
FLOWERING SEASON: late June through July. FLOWERS: white to pale pink, many, scattered 1 to 4 in axial clusters; about 1" (2.5 cm) long and wide, corolla trumpet-shaped. PLANT: trailing, 1–2½' (30–75 cm) long; leaves alternate, simple, arrowhead-shaped, margin entire, green. HABITAT: fields, meadows and waste areas. COMMENTS: often forms dense mats on the ground.

Biennial Gaura
• *Gaura biennis* L.
• Evening Primrose family **Onagraceae**
FLOWERING SEASON: July–August. FLOWERS: white turning pink just before wilting, few to several in small terminal clusters, nearly ½" (1.3 cm) wide, with 4 paddle-shaped petals all on the upper half of the flower, and 8 conspicuous drooping stamens. PLANT: 2–5' (0.6–1.5 m) tall; leaves alternate, simple, lance-shaped, margin shallowly toothed, green. HABITAT: in dry, sunny soils such as roadsides and fields.

Silverrod, White Goldenrod
• *Solidago bicolor*
• Aster family **Asteraceae**
FLOWERING SEASON: September into October. FLOWERS: white; flowerheads many in a 2–7" (5–17.5 cm) tall slender terminal or shorter upper axial clusters, up to ¼" (6 mm) wide, rimmed with usually 6 or 7 tiny petal-like rays. PLANT: 6–48" (15–120 cm) tall; leaves alternate, simple, obovate to oblong, pubescent, margin finely toothed, green. HABITAT: meadows, roadsides, and woodland borders.

Pearly Everlasting
• *Anaphalis margaritacea* (L.) Benth. and Hook. f. ex Clarke
• Aster family **Asteraceae**
FLOWERING SEASON: August. FLOWERS: white with a yellow center, flowerheads many, in dense 2–8" (5–20 cm) wide terminal and upper axial clusters, about ¼" (6 mm) wide, filamentous, surrounded by numerous pearly, petal-like bracts. PLANT: 1–3' (30–90 cm) tall; leaves alternate, simple, narrowly lance-shaped, pubescent above, woolly below, margin entire, pale green. HABITAT: fields, roadsides, woodland clearings, and waste areas.

Cassandra, Leatherleaf / *Chamaedaphne calyculata*

Silverrod, White Goldenrod / *Solidago bicolor*

Pearly Everlasting / *Anaphalis margaritacea*

Biennial Gaura / *Gaura biennis*

Field Bindweed / *Convolvulus arvensis*

Seneca Snakeroot / *Polygala senega*

Large Solomon's Seal

- *Polygonatum commutatum* (Schultes & Schultes) Dietr.
- Lily family **Liliaceae**

FLOWERING SEASON: late May to early June. FLOWERS: white with greenish tips, many, in axial clusters of 1 to 8, about ¾" (1.9 cm) long, tubularly bell-shaped with 6 small spreading tips, pendant. PLANT: 1–8' (0.3–2.4 m) long; leaves alternate, simple, broadly lance-shaped, margin entire, green. HABITAT: moist woodlands. COMMENTS: the common name Solomon's seal refers to circular stem scars found on the large root.

Small White Lady's Slipper

- *Cypripedium candidum* Muhl. ex Willd.
- Orchid family **Orchidaceae**

FLOWERING SEASON: late May to early June. FLOWERS: lip white, sepals and petals brownish green; 1 or occasionally 2, terminal, lip about 1" (2.5 cm) long, pouch-like. PLANT: 6–12" (15–30 cm) tall; leaves 3 or 4, alternate, simple, lance-shaped, margin entire, green. HABITAT: moist marl meadows. COMMENTS: *rare. Endangered. Do not disturb*. Only one population exists in New York State.

Lady's Slipper of the Queen

- *Cypripedium reginae* Walt.
- Orchid family **Orchidaceae**

FLOWERING SEASON: mid-June to the third week of July. FLOWERS: lip white with pinkish rose markings, sepals and petals white; 1 or 2, terminal; lip about 1 ¾" (4.5 cm) long, pouch-like. PLANT: 12–30" (30–75 cm) tall; leaves 3 to 7, alternate, simple, broadly ovate, margin entire, green. HABITAT: fens, swamps, moist meadows and woods. COMMENTS: the tallest of the New York lady's slippers.

White Fringed Orchid

- *Platanthera blephariglottis* (Willd.) Lindl.
- Orchid family **Orchidaceae**

FLOWERING SEASON: mid-July through August. FLOWERS: white, 10 to 20 or more, in a dense terminal cluster, about ⅜–⅝" (9–15 mm) long, with 5 small, petal-like parts and a large, single-lobed heavily fringed lip with a slender basal spur. PLANT: 12–24" (30–61 cm) tall; leaves alternate, simple, narrowly lance-shaped, margin entire, green. HABITAT: sphagnum fens and other open moist areas. COMMENTS: ragged fringed orchid, *Platanthera lacera*, has greenish white flowers with a 3-lobed, very deeply fringed lip.

Hooded Ladies'-tresses

- *Spiranthes romanzoffiana* Cham.
- Orchid family **Orchidaceae**

FLOWERING SEASON: late July through August. FLOWERS: white, 5 to 15 densely spiraled on a slender terminal cluster, about ⅜" (9 mm) long, appearing somewhat tubular, with 6 petal-like parts including the lip; lip deeply constricted about the middle. PLANT: 6–15" (15–37.5 cm) tall; leaves basal and alternate, simple, long and narrow, margin entire, green. HABITAT: usually in open moist to wet soils. COMMENTS: three other New York ladies'-tresses have flowers densely spiraled on the stem. Nodding ladies'-tresses, *Spiranthes cernua*, which flowers from late August through September, has ⅜" (9 mm) flowers and a shallowly constricted lip and is common in sunny fens and other moist soils. The physically similar creamy ladies'-tresses, *S. ochroleuca*, has white to off-white flowers, is found in drier shadier locations, and blooms from September into October. Wide-leaved ladies tresses, *S. lucida*, has flowers about ¼" (6 mm) long that are white with a bright yellow center and blooms in June and July.

Hooded Ladies'-tresses / *Spiranthes roman-zoffiana*

Small White Lady's Slipper / *Cypripedium candidum*

Lady's Slipper of the Queen / *Cypripedium reginae*

White Fringed Orchid / *Platanthera blephariglottis*

Large Solomon's Seal / *Polygonatum commutatum*

Tall White Bog Orchid, Bog Candle
•*Platanthera dilatata* (Pursh) Lindl.
  ex Beck
•Orchid family **Orchidaceae**
FLOWERING SEASON: mid-June through July. **FLOWERS:** white, up to 100 in a dense slender terminal cluster, about ⅖–⁷⁄₁₀" (10–18 mm) wide, with 6 spreading, petal-like parts, including a lip with a slender basal spur; pleasantly fragrant. **PLANT:** 12–24" (30–60 cm) tall; leaves alternate, simple, narrowly lance-shaped, margin entire, green. **HABITAT:** fens and moist meadows.

LEAVES ALTERNATE, COMPOUND OR DEEPLY DIVIDED

Red Baneberry
•*Actaea spicata* L. ssp. *rubra* (Ait.)
  Hulten
•Crowfoot family **Ranunculaceae**
FLOWERING SEASON: mid-to late May. **FLOWERS:** white, many in a showy rounded terminal cluster about 1¼" (3.1 cm) wide, individual flowers about ¼" (6 mm) wide with many thread-like stamens and 4 to 10 narrow, inconspicuous petals. **PLANT:** 1–2' (30–60 cm) tall; leaves alternate, compound with 9 to 15 leaflets; leaflets variable, margins sharply and unevenly toothed, green; fruit a cylindrical cluster of oval red berries. **HABITAT:** woodlands. **COMMENTS:** white baneberry, *A. pachypoda*, also known as doll's eyes, has oval white berries with a prominent black terminal spot.

Tall Meadow-rue
•*Thalictrum pubescens* Pursh
•Crowfoot family **Ranunculaceae**
FLOWERING SEASON: mid-June through July. **FLOWERS:** white, many, in showy terminal clusters, about ⁵⁄₁₆" (8 mm) wide, composed of a rounded fluffy mass of thread-like stamens. **PLANT:** about 3–10' (1–3 m) tall; leaves alternate, compound with numerous leaflets; leaflets somewhat oblong with up to 3 shallow lobes, margin entire, green. **HABITAT:** open, sunny swamps.

Black Snakeroot
•*Cimicifuga racemosa* (L.) Nutt.
•Crowfoot family **Ranunculaceae**
FLOWERING SEASON: July. **FLOWERS:** white, many, in showy slender terminal clusters up to 2 feet long, about ½" (1.3 cm) wide, composed of rounded clusters of thread-like stamens and 4 to 8 inconspicuous petals; disagreeable fragrance. **PLANT:** about 3–8' (1–2.4 m) tall; leaves alternate, compound with numerous leaflets; leaflets variable, margins sharply and unevenly toothed, green. **HABITAT:** woodlands.

Canadian Burnet
•*Sanguisorba canadensis* L.
•Rose family **Rosaceae**
FLOWERING SEASON: August–September. **FLOWERS:** white, many, in slender 1–6" (2.5–15 cm) cylindrical terminal clusters; about ¼" (6 mm) wide, with 4 prominent filamentous stamens over 4 inconspicuous petal-like parts. **PLANT:** 1–6' (0.3–1.8 m) tall; leaves alternate, pinnately compound with 7 to 15 leaflets; leaflets narrowly ovate, margins toothed, green. **HABITAT:** swamps and moist meadows

White Sweet-clover
•*Melilotus alba* Desr. Ex Lam.
•Bean family **Fabaceae**
FLOWERING SEASON: June–August. **FLOWERS:** white, many in slender 2–4" (5–10 cm) long, often 1-sided axial clusters, about ¼" (6 mm) long, narrowly pea-like. **PLANT:** 3–9' (1–2.7 m) tall; leaves alternate, compound with 3 leaflets; leaflets narrowly oblong, margin toothed, green. **HABITAT:** fields, roadsides, and waste areas.

Tall White Bog Orchid, Bog Candle / *Platanthera dilatata*

Black Snakeroot / *Cimicifuga racemosa*

White Sweet-clover / *Melilotus alba*

Red Baneberry / *Actaea spicata* ssp. *rubra*

Canadian Burnet / *Sanguisorba canadensis*

Tall Meadow-rue / *Thalictrum pubescens*

LEAVES OPPOSITE OR WHORLED, SIMPLE

Wild Hydrangea

- *Hydrangea arborescens* L.
- Hydrangea family **Hydrangeaceae**

FLOWERING SEASON: July. FLOWERS: white, many in 2–5" (5–12.5 cm) rounded terminal clusters, about $^3/_{16}$" (5 mm) wide, with 8 to 10 showy thread-like stamens. PLANT: shrub, 2–8' (0.6–2.4 m) tall; leaves opposite, simple, broadly ovate with a pointed tip, margin toothed, green. HABITAT: rocky woodlands. COMMENTS: *protected. Endangered. Do not disturb.* In New York largely confined to the south-central Finger Lakes area near the Pennsylvania border.

Enchanter's Nightshade

- *Circaea lutetiana* L.
- Evening Primrose family **Onagraceae**

FLOWERING SEASON: July–August. FLOWERS: white, several, in slender terminal clusters, about $^3/_{16}$" (5 mm) wide, with 2 rounded, notched petals. PLANT: 1–2' (30–60 cm) tall; leaves opposite, simple, ovate, margin shallowly toothed, green. HABITAT: woodlands and waste areas. COMMENTS: small enchanter's nightshade, *C. alpina*, is nearly identical but is smaller, up to 8" (20 cm) tall, and has somewhat more coarsely toothed leaves.

Eyebright

- *Euphrasia stricta* Wolff ex Lehm.
- Figwort family **Scrophulariaceae**

FLOWERING SEASON: August–September. FLOWERS: white to pinkish white with a yellow center and purple veining, few to several in short terminal clusters, about $^1/_4$–$^3/_8$" (6–9 mm) long, tubular and 2-lipped; upper lip 2-lobed; lower lip with 3 deeply notched lobes. PLANT: 4–10" (10–25 cm) tall; leaves opposite, simple, ovate, margin coarsely toothed, green. HABITAT: fields and open hillsides.

Cow-wheat

- *Melampyrum lineare* Desr.
- Figwort family **Scrophulariaceae**

FLOWERING SEASON: late June into August. FLOWERS: white with a yellow lower lip, several, found in pairs in axils, up to $^1/_2$" (1.3 cm) long, tubular with 2 short lips. PLANT: 6–18" (15–45 cm) tall; leaves opposite, simple, narrowly lance-shaped, margin entire or with 2 or 3 pairs of sharply pointed teeth near the base, green. HABITAT: woodlands and thickets.

Turtle-heads

- *Chelone glabra* L.
- Figwort family **Scrophulariaceae**

FLOWERING SEASON: late July to early September. FLOWERS: white to faintly pink, several in a terminal cluster; about 1" (2.5 cm) long, tubular and 2-lipped; upper lip large and hood-shaped; lower lip 3-lobed. PLANT: about 1–3' (30–90 cm) tall; leaves opposite, simple, lance-shaped, margin toothed, green. HABITAT: swamps, fens, and along streams.

Culver's-root

- *Veronicastrum virginicum* (L.) Farw.
- Figwort family **Scrophulariaceae**

FLOWERING SEASON: August. FLOWERS: white, many, in densely flowered slender 3–9" (7.5–22.5 cm) long terminal clusters; individual flowers about $^3/_{16}$" (5 mm) long, tubular with 4 tiny lobes. PLANT: 2–7' (0.6–2.1 m) tall; leaves whorled in groups of 3 to 9, simple, lance-shaped, margin sharply toothed, green. HABITAT: moist meadows and woodlands.

Wild Hydrangea / *Hydrangea arborescens*

Enchanter's Nightshade / *Circaea lute-tiana*

Culver's-root / *Veronicastrum virginicum*

Eyebright / *Euphrasia stricta*

Cow-wheat / *Melampyrum lineare*

Turtle-heads / *Chelone glabra*

Water-willow
•*Justicia americana* (L.) Vahl
•Acanthus family **Acanthaceae**
FLOWERING SEASON: July to early August.
FLOWERS: white with violet markings, 2
to 4, in long-stalked axial clusters, about
½" (1.3 cm) long, tubular and 2-lipped;
upper lip erect; lower lip with 3 large,
spreading, petal-like lobes. PLANT: about
1–3' (30–90 cm) tall; leaves opposite,
simple, long and narrow, margin entire,
green. HABITAT: aquatic (in shallow
water).

Buttonbush
•*Cephalanthus occidentalis* L
•Madder family **Rubiaceae**
FLOWERING SEASON: mid-July to mid-
August. FLOWERS: white, many, in densely flowered, 1" (2.5 cm) wide spherical
terminal flowerheads, about ⁷⁄₁₆" (1.1 cm)
long, tubular with 4 tiny, sharply pointed
lobes. PLANT: shrub, 3–12' (0.9–4 m)
tall; leaves whorled or opposite, simple,
ovate with a pointed tip, margin entire,
green. HABITAT: swamps and moist
meadows.

White Snakeroot
•*Eupatorium rugosum* Houtt.
•Aster family **Asteraceae**
FLOWERING SEASON: mid-July to mid-
September. FLOWERS: white, flowerheads many, in dense, flat-topped terminal clusters, up to ³⁄₁₆" (5 mm) long, filamentous. PLANT: 1–5' (0.3–1.5 m) tall;
leaves opposite, simple, ovate with a
pointed tip, margin toothed, green.
HABITAT: woodlands.

Boneset
•*Eupatorium perfoliatum* L.
•Aster family **Asteraceae**
FLOWERING SEASON: August to late
September. FLOWERS: white, flower-
heads many, in dense terminal clusters,
about ¼" (6 mm) long, filamentous.

PLANT: 2–5' (0.6–1.5 m) tall; leaves
opposite, simple, joined and perfoliate at
the base, lance-shaped, margin toothed,
green. HABITAT: wet soil in fields, roadsides, and waste areas.

LEAVES OPPOSITE, COMPOUND OR DEEPLY LOBED

Garden Valerian
•*Valeriana officinalis* L.
•Valerian family **Valerianaceae**
FLOWERING SEASON: June–July. FLOW-
ERS: pinkish white to off-white, many, in
showy rounded terminal clusters, about
⅛" (4 mm) long, tubular with 5 petal-like
lobes. PLANT: 2–5' (0.6–1.5 m) tall;
leaves opposite, simple, deeply and pinnately divided into 7 to 15 or more narrow lobes, margins sharply toothed,
green. HABITAT: fields and roadsides.

Buttonbush / *Cephalanthus occidentalis*

Water-willow / *Justicia americana*

White Snakeroot / *Eupatorium rugosum*

Garden Valerian / *Valeriana officinalis*

Boneset / *Eupatorium perfoliatum*

PART TWO

PINK TO RED FLOWERS
INCLUDING REDDISH PURPLE
❧

FLOWERS SYMMETRICAL, WITH 3 PETALS OR PETAL-LIKE PARTS

LEAVES WHORLED, SIMPLE

Purple Trillium
- *Trillium erectum* L.
- Lily family **Liliaceae**

FLOWERING SEASON: late April through May. FLOWER: purplish red, solitary, terminal on an erect stalk, about 2½" (6.3 cm) wide, with 3 evenly whorled petals; petals lance-shaped, often slightly recurved. PLANT: 8–16" (20–40 cm) tall; leaves 3 in a whorl at the base of the flower stalk, simple, broadly ovate with a pointed tip, stalkless, margin entire, green. HABITAT: woodlands. COMMENTS: a form with greenish-yellow petals is fairly common. Odor unpleasant, like a wet dog.

Toad-shade
- *Trillium sessile* L.
- Lily family **Liliaceae**

FLOWERING SEASON: mid-to late May. FLOWER: maroon or occasionally greenish-yellow, solitary, stalkless, about 2" (5 cm) tall, with 3 erect, narrowly lance-shaped petals. PLANT: 4–12" (10–30 cm) tall; leaves 3, in a whorl at the base of the flower, simple, ovate with an entire margin, stalkless, dark green often mottled with lighter green. HABITAT: moist woodlands. COMMENTS: *protected. Endangered. Do not disturb*. Known only in New York from the western regions of the state.

FLOWERS SYMMETRICAL, WITH 4 PETALS OR PETAL-LIKE PARTS

LEAVES ALTERNATE, SIMPLE

Dame's Rocket
- *Hesperis matronalis* L.

- Mustard family **Brassicaceae**

FLOWERING SEASON: late May through June. FLOWERS: white, pink, purplish or variegated, many, in axial and terminal clusters, about ¾" (2 cm) wide, cross-shaped, with 4 rounded petals. PLANT: 2–3' (60–90 cm) tall; leaves alternate, simple, broadly lance-shaped, margin minutely toothed, green; seed pods up to 4" (10 cm) long, slender. HABITAT: fields, roadsides, waste areas, and woodlands.

Daphne
- *Daphne mezereum* L.
- Mezereum family **Thymelaeaceae**

FLOWERING SEASON: mid-April to early May. FLOWERS: rose-purple to occasionally white, many, in clusters of 2 to 5 along the branches, about ½" (1.3 cm) long, tubular with 4 spreading, petal-like lobes; pleasantly fragrant. PLANT: shrub, 1–4' (0.3–1.2 m) tall; leaves alternate and mostly clustered near branch tips, simple, lance-shaped, margin entire, green. HABITAT: moist woodlands.

Fireweed
- *Epilobium angustifolium* L.
- Evening Primrose family **Onagraceae**

FLOWERING SEASON: mid-July through August. FLOWERS: pinkish purple, many in a slender, pyramid-shaped terminal cluster, about 1" (2.5 cm) wide, with 4 rounded, unequal petals. PLANT: 2–8' (0.6–2.4 m) tall; leaves alternate, simple, lance-shaped, margin entire, green. HABITAT: roadsides, fields, or recently disturbed or burned areas.

Great Hairy Willow-herb
- *Epilobium hirsutum* L.
- Evening Primrose family **Onagraceae**

FLOWERING SEASON: mid-July through August. FLOWERS: rose-purple, several in a terminal cluster, about 1" (2.5 cm) wide, with 4 rounded, distinctly notched petals. PLANT: 2–5' (0.6–1.5 m) tall;

Toad-shade / *Trillium sessile*

Purple Trillium / *Trillium erectum*

Daphne / *Daphne mezereum*

Great Hairy Willow-herb / *Epilobium hirsutum*

Fireweed / *Epilobium angustifolium*

Dame's Rocket / *Hesperis matronalis*

leaves alternate, simple, lance-shaped, margin sharply toothed, green. HABITAT: open moist areas and waste areas.

LEAVES OPPOSITE, SIMPLE

Meadow-beauty
•*Rhexia virginica* L.
•Melastome family **Melastomaceae**
FLOWERING SEASON: mid-August into September. FLOWERS: pinkish purple, few to several, terminal, about 1¼" (3.1 cm) wide, with 4 rounded petals and 8 conspicuous bright yellow stamens. PLANT: 12–18" (30–45 cm) tall; leaves opposite, simple, broadly lance-shaped, margin toothed, green. HABITAT: moist sandy soils, frequently near the ocean but also found inland. COMMENTS: deer-grass, *Rhexia mariana*, which has paler flowers and narrower leaves is typically restricted to the southeastern part of New York.

FLOWERS SYMMETRICAL, WITH 5 PETALS OR PETAL-LIKE PARTS

LEAVES BASAL, SIMPLE

Pitcher-plant
•*Sarracenia purpurea* L.
•Pitcher-plant family **Sarraceniaceae**
FLOWERING SEASON: June. FLOWER: purplish red with a yellowish shield-like center, solitary, terminal, about 2" (5 cm) wide, with 5 obovate petals that are narrowed in the middle, nodding. PLANT: 8–24" (20–60 cm) tall; leaves basal, simple, tubular, pitcher-like with downward-pointing stiff hairs on the inner surface, green to red with purple veining. HABITAT: bogs and fens. COMMENTS: a carnivorous plant.

Pink Pyrola
•*Pyrola asarifolia* Michx.
•Shinleaf family **Pyrolaceae**

FLOWERING SEASON: mid-June to mid-July. FLOWERS: rose to pale purple, several to many in a spike-like terminal cluster, about ⅝" (1.6 cm) wide, with 5 rounded petals, nodding. PLANT: 5–10" (12.5–25 cm) tall; leaves basal, simple, broadly kidney-shaped to nearly round, margin minutely toothed, green. HABITAT: moist woodlands, swamps, and fens. COMMENTS: *protected. Threatened. Do not disturb.*

LEAVES ALTERNATE, SIMPLE

Smartweed
•*Polygonum pensylvanicum* L.
•Buckwheat family **Polygonaceae**
FLOWERING SEASON: August–September. FLOWERS: pinkish white to rose, many in densely flowered, cylindrical terminal clusters, minute with 5 petal-like lobes. PLANT: 1–3' (30–90 cm) tall; leaves alternate, simple, lance-shaped, margin entire, green. HABITAT: fields, cultivated ground, and moist soil. COMMENTS: many species of smartweed, some with arrowhead-shaped leaves and *painfully prickly stems,* are found in New York.

Rose Mallow
•*Hibiscus moscheutos* L.
•Mallow family **Malvaceae**
FLOWERING SEASON: late July through August. FLOWERS: pink or white often with a crimson center, 1–several, mostly terminal, 4–7" (10–17.5 cm) wide, with 5 broad, rounded petals. PLANT: 4–7' (1.2–2.1 m) tall; leaves alternate, simple, ovate with a pointed tip, lower leaves sometimes 3-lobed, margin finely toothed, green. HABITAT: brackish marshes, most often in coastal areas but occasionally in large inland swamps, such as Montezuma.

Pink Pyrola / *Pyrola asarifolia*

Smartweed / *Polygonum pensylvanicum*

Pitcher-plant / *Sarracenia purpurea*

Rose Mallow / *Hibiscus moscheutos*

Meadow-beauty / *Rhexia virginica*

Hardhack

- *Spiraea tomentosa* L.
- Rose family **Rosaceae**

FLOWERING SEASON: mid-July to mid-August. **FLOWERS:** rosy pink, many in upright 3–5" (7.5–12.5 cm) tall upper axial and terminal clusters, about ⁵⁄₁₆" (8 mm) wide, with 5 rounded petals. **PLANT:** shrub, 2–4' (0.6–1.2 m) tall; leaves alternate, simple, oval to oblong, margin coarsely and unevenly toothed, green, woolly on the lower surface. **HABITAT:** swamps and open moist ground.

Purple-flowering Raspberry

- *Rubus odoratus* L.
- Rose family **Rosaceae**

FLOWERING SEASON: June–July. **FLOWERS:** pink to pale purple, few to several in terminal and upper axial clusters, 1–2" (2.5–5 cm) wide, with 5 rounded petals. **PLANT:** shrub, 2–5' (0.6–1.5 m) tall; leaves alternate, simple, maple-like, 3 to 5-lobed; lobes pointed, margins irregularly toothed, green; upper limbs coated with purplish hairs. **HABITAT:** along the edges of woods, streams, trails and roadsides.

Lapland Rosebay

- *Rhododendron lapponicum* (L.) Wahl.
- Heath family **Ericaceae**

FLOWERING SEASON: June. **FLOWERS:** pinkish purple, usually 1 to 4 in a loose terminal cluster, about ¾" (1.9 cm) wide, tubular at the base with 5 spreading, petal-like lobes. **PLANT:** mostly prostrate; leaves alternate, mostly clustered near the tips of woody stems, simple, lance-shaped with an entire margin, green, evergreen. **COMMENTS:** *protected. Endangered. Do not disturb.*

Live-forever

- *Sedum telephium* L.
- Sedum family **Crassulaceae**

FLOWERING SEASON: August–September. **FLOWERS:** pinkish red to reddish purple, many in flat-topped, circular terminal clusters, about ¼" (7 mm) wide, with 5 lance-shaped petals. **PLANT:** 12–18" (30–45 cm) tall; leaves alternate, simple, ovate, thick and fleshy, margin coarsely toothed, light green. **HABITAT:** fields, roadsides, and moist areas.

LEAVES ALTERNATE, COMPOUND OR DEEPLY DIVIDED

Musk-mallow

- *Malva moschata* L.
- Mallow family **Malvaceae**

FLOWERING SEASON: mid-June through July. **FLOWERS:** pink or white, often with lavender veins, several, most in terminal clusters, 1½–2" (3.8–5 cm) wide, with 5 broad petals notched at the tip. **PLANT:** 1–2' (30–60 cm) tall; leaves alternate, simple, with 5 deeply cut and subdivided lobes, green. **HABITAT:** fields, roadsides, and waste areas. **COMMENTS:** the high mallow, *Malva sylvestris*, has reddish purple flowers and maple-like leaves.

Queen-of-the-Prairie

- *Filipendula rubra* (Hill) B. Robinson
- Rose family **Rosaceae**

FLOWERING SEASON: July. **FLOWERS:** pink, many in a large showy terminal cluster, about ⁵⁄₁₆" (8 mm) wide, with 5 rounded petals, fragrant. **PLANT:** 2–8' (0.6–2.4 m) tall; leaves alternate, pinnately compound; leaflets deeply divided, ovate to lance-shaped, margins toothed, green. **HABITAT:** moist meadows.

Queen-of-the-prairie / *Filipendula rubra*

Purple-flowering Raspberry / *Rubus odoratus*

Musk-mallow / *Malva moschata*

Lapland Rosbay / *Rhododendron lapponicum*

Hardhack / *Spiraea tomentosa*

Live-forever / *Sedum telephium*

Sea-beach Rose, Salt-spray Rose

•*Rosa rugosa* Thunb.

•Rose family **Rosaceae**

FLOWERING SEASON: July–August. FLOW-ERS: dark rose-pink to rose-lavender with a yellow center, solitary to several in leaf axils, 2–3" (5–7.5 cm) wide, with 5 rounded petals, fragrant. PLANT: shrub, 2–5' (0.6–1.5 m) tall; leaves alternate, pinnately compound with 5 to 9 leaflets; leaflets elliptic to oblong, margins toothed, green; stem very spiny and hairy; fruit a large, rounded red hip. HABITAT: thickets, sand dunes and road-sides near the ocean.

Purple Avens, Water Avens

•*Geum rivale* L.

•Rose family **Rosaceae**

FLOWERING SEASON: mid-May to mid-June. FLOWERS: purple, few in a loose terminal cluster, ¾–1" (1.9–2.5 cm) wide, urn-shaped, with 5 rounded petals, nodding. PLANT: about 1–3' (30–90 cm) tall; leaves alternate, pinnate-ly compound; leaflets ovate to lance-shaped, margins toothed, green. HABI-TAT: swamps and low moist ground.

Purple Cinquefoil, Marsh Cinque-foil

•*Potentilla palustris* (L.) Scop.

•Rose family **Rosaceae**

FLOWERING SEASON: July. FLOWERS: pur-ple, solitary to several, terminal or axil-lary, ¾–1¼" (1.9–3.1 cm) wide, with 5 tiny petals alternating with 5 larger pointed, petal-like sepals. PLANT: trail-ing, up to 2' (60 cm) or more long; leaves alternate, pinnately compound; leaflets oblong to oval, margins toothed, green. HABITAT: swamps, fens, and bogs.

LEAVES OPPOSITE OR WHORLED, SIMPLE OR DEEPLY DIVIDED

Deptford Pink

•*Dianthus armeria* L.

•Pink family **Caryophyllaceae**

FLOWERING SEASON: mid-June to early August. FLOWERS: pink with white dots, one to few in small terminal groups, about ½" (1.3 cm) wide, with 5 elliptical petals that are finely toothed at the tips. PLANT: 6–18" (15–45 cm) tall; leaves opposite, simple, long and narrow, mar-gin entire, green. HABITAT: fields and woodland edges.

Ragged-robin

•*Lychnis flos-cuculi* L.

•Pink family **Caryophyllaceae**

FLOWERING SEASON: late May to mid-June. FLOWERS: pink, several to many, in terminal and upper axial clusters, about ¾" (2 cm) wide, with 5 petals, each petal cleft into 4 long narrow lobes. PLANT: 1–2' (30–60 cm) tall; leaves basal and opposite, simple, narrowly lance-shaped, margin entire, green. HABITAT: moist fields and meadows.

Sheep Laurel, Lambkill

•*Kalmia angustifolia* L.

•Heath family **Ericaceae**

FLOWERING SEASON: late May to early July. FLOWERS: dark reddish pink, many in a spherical cluster on the upper por-tion of the stems, about ½" (1.2 cm) wide, saucer-shaped with 5 shallowly pointed lobes. PLANT: shrub, 6–36" (15–90 cm) tall; leaves opposite or in whorls of 3, simple, narrowly oblong with an entire margin, green, evergreen. HABITAT: in moist soils along wood-lands, swamps, and fens. COMMENTS: *the alternate common name lambkill refers to the poisonous nature of this plant.*

Purple Cinquefoil, Marsh Cinquefoil / *Potentilla palustris*

Ragged-robin / *Lychnis flos-cuculi*

Sea-beach Rose, Salt-spray Rose / *Rosa rugosa*

Deptford Pink / *Dianthus armeria*

Purple Avens, Water Avens / *Geum rivale*

Sheep Laurel, Lambkill / *Kalmia angustifolia*

Alpine Azalea

•*Loiseleuria procumbens* (L.) Desv.
•Heath family **Ericaceae**
FLOWERING SEASON: June. **FLOWERS**: pink to white, 1 to 5 in loose terminal groups, about ³⁄₁₆" (5 mm) long, short-tubular with 5 large triangular lobes. **PLANT**: nearly prostrate; leaves mostly opposite along a woody stem, simple, narrowly elliptic with an incurved margin, green, evergreen. **HABITAT**: alpine regions of the Adirondack Mountains. **COMMENTS**: *protected. Endangered. Do not disturb.*

Wild Geranium

•*Geranium maculatum* L.
•Geranium family **Geraniaceae**
FLOWERING SEASON: mid-May to mid-June. **FLOWERS**: rose-purple to occasionally white, 1 to 3 in loose terminal clusters, about 1¼" (3.1 cm) wide, with 5 rounded petals. **PLANT**: 1–2' (30–60 cm) tall; leaves basal and opposite along the stem, simple, deeply divided into 5 lobes, margin unevenly toothed, green. **HABITAT**: woodlands.

Herb-robert

•*Geranium robertianum* L.
•Geranium family **Geraniaceae**
FLOWERING SEASON: late May into September. **FLOWERS**: dark pink to reddish purple, several in pairs on axial stalks, about ½" (1.3 cm) wide, with 5 rounded petals. **PLANT**: 6–18" (15–45 cm) tall; leaves opposite, deeply and repeatedly divided, margins finely lobed or toothed, green. **HABITAT**: woodlands.

Sea-pink, Marsh-pink

•*Sabatia stellaris* Pursh.
•Gentian family **Gentianaceae**
FLOWERING SEASON: August. **FLOWERS**: pink with a yellow center bordered in red, several, terminal, about 1" (2.5 cm) wide, corolla with 5 oval petal-like lobes. **PLANT**: 6–24" (15–60 cm) tall; leaves opposite, simple, narrow, margin entire, green. **HABITAT**: salt meadows. **COMMENTS**: *protected. Threatened. Do not disturb.* The slender marsh-pink, *Sabatia campanulata*, has narrow green sepals the length of the petals; rose pink, *S. angularis*, extremely rare in New York, has a 4-angled lower stem. The large marsh-pink, *S. dodecandra*, possibly extinct in New York, has flowers about 2" (5 cm) wide with 8 to 12 petal-like parts.

Common Milkweed

•*Asclepias syriaca* L.
•Milkweed family **Asclepiadaceae**
FLOWERING SEASON: late June to mid-July. **FLOWERS**: greenish, purple to pinkish white, many in rounded terminal or upper axial clusters, about ³⁄₈" (1 cm) wide, with 5 deeply recurved petals and a 5-pointed crown-like center. **PLANT**: 3–5' (0.9–1.5 m) tall; leaves opposite, simple, oblong, margin entire, green. **HABITAT**: fields and waste areas.

Spreading Dogbane

•*Apocynum androsaemifolium* L.
•Dogbane family **Apocynaceae**
FLOWERING SEASON: late June through July. **FLOWERS**: pink, several to many, in loose terminal or axial clusters, about ⁵⁄₁₆" (8 mm) wide, bell-shaped with 5 tooth-like lobes. **PLANT**: 1–4' (0.3–1.2 m) tall; leaves opposite, simple, oval, margin entire, green. **HABITAT**: moist fields and meadows. **COMMENTS**: plant exudes a milky white latex when cut.

Herb-Robert / *Geranium robertianum*

Alpine Azalea / *Loiseleuria procumbens*

Common Milkweed / *Asclepias syriaca*

Wild Geranium / *Geranium maculatum*

Spreading Dogbane / *Apocynum andro-saemifolium*

Sea-pink, Marsh-pink / *Sabatia stellaris*

Summer Phlox

- *Phlox paniculata* L.
- Phlox family **Polemoniaceae**

FLOWERING SEASON: mid-July into September. **FLOWERS:** pink, purple, or white, many in dense, rounded terminal and axial clusters, about 1" (2.5 cm) wide, tubular with 5 nearly round, overlapping, petal-like lobes; fragrant. **PLANT:** 2–5' (0.6–1.5 m) tall; leaves opposite, simple, lance-shaped, margin entire, green. **HABITAT:** meadows and open woodlots. **COMMENTS:** *Phlox maculata* is a shorter plant with smaller flowers and purple-spotted stems.

Twinflower

- *Linnaea borealis* L.
- Honeysuckle family **Caprifoliaceae**

FLOWERING SEASON: mid-June to mid-July. **FLOWERS:** pinkish, in pairs on tall terminal stalks, about ⁷⁄₁₆" (1.1 cm) long, bell-shaped with 5 petal-like lobes, nodding. **PLANT:** prostrate; leaves opposite on 6–15" (15–37.5 cm) long stems, simple, ovate, margin scalloped, green. **HABITAT:** woodland clearings, shaded fens, and along woodland streams.

~

FLOWERS SYMMETRICAL, WITH 6 PETALS OR PETAL-LIKE PARTS

LEAVES ALTERNATE, SIMPLE

Twisted-stalk, Rose Mandarin

- *Streptopus roseus* Michx.
- Lily family **Liliaceae**

FLOWERING SEASON: mid-May to early June. **FLOWERS:** purplish rose, several, found singly or occasionally paired in axils, about ½" (1.3 cm) long, bell-shaped with 6 sharply pointed often recurved tips, pendant. **PLANT:** 1–2½' (30–75 cm) tall; leaves alternate along an angularly twisted stalk, simple, lance-shaped with a rounded base slightly clasping the stem, margin entire, green. **HABITAT:** moist woodlands. **COMMENTS:** the common name twisted-stalk refers to the zigzag appearance of the stalk.

LEAVES OPPOSITE OR WHORLED, SIMPLE

Swamp Loosestrife

- *Decodon verticillatus* (L.) Ell.
- Loosestrife family **Lythraceae**

FLOWERING SEASON: August. **FLOWERS:** pinkish purple, many, in crowded axial clusters, about 1" (2.5 cm) wide, with 6 narrow petals. **PLANT:** 3–10' (0.9–3 m) tall; leaves whorled, simple, narrowly lance-shaped, margin entire, green. **HABITAT:** swamps.

Purple Loosestrife

- *Lythrum salicaria* L.
- Loosestrife family **Lythraceae**

FLOWERING SEASON: July into August. **FLOWERS:** purplish pink to reddish purple, many, in tall, slender terminal clusters, about ⅝" (1.6 cm) wide, with 6 petals. **PLANT:** 2–4' (0.6–1.2 m) tall; leaves mostly opposite, simple, lance-shaped, margin entire, green. **HABITAT:** swamps, roadsides, and moist soils. **COMMENTS:** an introduced ornamental that has become a serious wetland invader.

Twinflower / *Linnaea borealis*

Purple Loosestrife / *Lythrum salicaria*

Swamp Loosestrife / *Decodon verticillatus*

Summer Phlox / *Phlox paniculata*

Twisted-stalk, Rose Mandarin / *Streptopus roseus*

FLOWERS SYMMETRICAL, WITH 7 OR MORE PETALS OR PETAL-LIKE PARTS

LEAVES ALTERNATE, SIMPLE

Robin's-plantain

•*Erigeron pulchellus* Michx.

•Aster family **Asteraceae**

FLOWERING SEASON: late May to early June. FLOWERS: pale violet or purplish with a yellow center, flowerheads 1 to 6 in a terminal cluster, 1–1½" (2.5–3.8 cm) wide, rimmed with numerous very narrow, petal-like rays. PLANT: 10–24" (25–60 cm) tall; leaves alternate and basal, simple to lance-shaped, margin finely toothed, green. HABITAT: open woodlands and shaped roadsides.

New England Aster

•*Aster novae-angliae* L.

•Aster family **Asteraceae**

FLOWERING SEASON: mid-August into October. FLOWERS: violet-purple with a yellow center, flowerheads many, terminal and upper axial, 1–2" (2.5–5 cm) wide, rimmed with 40 to 50 petal-like rays. PLANT: 2–8' (0.6–2.4 m) tall; leaves alternate, simple, lance-shaped, margin entire, green. HABITAT: meadows, roadsides, and along swamps.

LEAVES OPPOSITE, COMPOUND OR DEEPLY DIVIDED

Field Scabious, Bluebuttons

•*Knautia arvensis* (L.) Coulter

•Teasel family **Dipsacaceae**

FLOWERING SEASON: June–July. FLOWERS: lilac-purple, flowerheads many, terminal and upper axial, about 1¼" (3.1 cm) wide, composed of many multi-lobed petal-like rays. PLANT: 1–3' (30–90 cm) tall; leaves basal or opposite, simple, lance-shaped to 5–7 lobed, margin entire, green. HABITAT: fields and waste areas.

FLOWERS NOT RADIALLY SYMMETRICAL; FLOWERS MINUTE, FILAMENTOUS, TUBULAR WITH NO PETAL-LIKE LOBES, OR WITH NO OBVIOUS PETAL-LIKE PARTS

LEAF ABSENT OR TYPICALLY LACKING AT FLOWERING

Pinesap, False Beechdrops

•*Monotropa hypopithys* L.

•Indian-pipe family **Monotropaceae**

FLOWERING SEASON: July–August. FLOWERS: white, yellowish or pink, several in a 1-sided terminal cluster, about ½" (1.3 cm) long, appearing tubular, with usually 5 slightly flaring tips, nodding. PLANT: 4–12" (10–30 cm) tall; leaves absent; stalk with numerous tiny leaf-like bracts, white, yellowish, or pink. HABITAT: woodlands.

Cranefly Orchid

•*Tipularia discolor* (Pursh) Nutt.

•Orchid family **Orchidaceae**

FLOWERING SEASON: late July through mid-August. FLOWERS: greenish lavender with purplish mottling, 30 to 50 in a slender terminal cluster, about ½" (1.3 cm) tall and wide, with 6 petal-like parts, including a lip with a slender, about ⅘" (2 cm) long spur. PLANT: 15–20" (38–50 cm) tall; leaf solitary, basal, simple, broadly obovate, margin entire, green, with purplish mottling, not present at flowering. HABITAT: sandy woodlands. COMMENTS: *protected. Endangered. Do not disturb.* In New York, restricted to one area of Long Island.

New England Aster / *Aster novae-angliae*

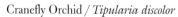

Pinesap, False Beech-drops / *Monotropa hypopithys*

Cranefly Orchid / *Tipularia discolor*

Robin's-plantain / *Erigeron pulchellus*

Field Scabious, Bluebuttons / *Knautia arvensis*

LEAVES BASAL, SIMPLE

Moccasin Flower, Pink Lady's Slipper

- *Cypripedium acaule* Ait.
- Orchid family **Orchidaceae**

FLOWERING SEASON: late May through June. FLOWERS: lip pink, sepals and petals light purplish brown; solitary, terminal; lip about 2" (5 cm) long and pouch-like, pendant. PLANT: 6–12" (15–30 cm) tall; leaves 2, basal, simple, broadly oblong, margin entire, green. HABITAT: variable, from dry coniferous or mixed woods to sphagnum fens. COMMENTS: the most commonly encountered lady's slipper in New York.

Showy Orchis

- *Galearis spectabilis* (L.) Raf.
- Orchid family **Orchidaceae**

FLOWERING SEASON: late May through late June. FLOWERS: bicolored, pale purplish and white, 3 to 6 on a slender terminal cluster, about 1" (2.5 cm) tall; 5 sepals and petals, pale purplish, overlapping and hood-like; lip white, pendant, obovate with a prominent spur. PLANT: 4–12" (10–30 cm) tall; leaves 2, basal, simple, obovate, margin entire, green. HABITAT: woodlands.

Calopogon, Grass Pink

- *Calopogon tuberosus* (L.) BSP.
- Orchid family **Orchidaceae**

FLOWERING SEASON: late June through late July. FLOWERS: pink to rose pink, 3 to 15 in a slender terminal cluster, about 1¼" (3.1 cm) tall and wide, with 5 oblong to obovate petals and sepals and an erect lip; lip narrow, triangular-tipped, with a conspicuous tuft of white to yellow-tipped hairs. PLANT: 1–2½" (2.5–6.3 cm) tall; leaf usually solitary, basal, simple, long and narrow, green, margin entire. HABITAT: sphagnum fens.

LEAVES BASAL, COMPOUND OR DEEPLY DIVIDED

Indian-paint Brush

- *Castilleja coccinea* (L.) Spreng.
- Figwort family **Scrophulariaceae**

FLOWERING SEASON: June–July. FLOWERS: appearing scarlet, many, terminal, about 1" (2.5 cm) long, corolla tubular, greenish yellow but hidden by 3- to 5-lobed bright scarlet floral bracts. PLANT: 1–2' (30–60 cm) tall; leaves of two types, basal leaves oblong, stem leaves alternate, 3-to 5-lobed, green. HABITAT: meadows and moist thickets. COMMENTS: *protected. Endangered. Do not disturb.*

LEAVES ALTERNATE, SIMPLE

Early Azalea

- *Rhododendron prinophyllum* (Small) Millais
- Heath family **Ericaceae**

FLOWERING SEASON: mid-May to mid-June. FLOWERS: pale pink, several in a terminal cluster, about 2" (5 cm) long, tubular at the base with 5 unequal and widely flaring lobes, extremely fragrant. PLANT: shrub, 2–6' (0.6–1.8 m) tall; leaves alternate, mostly clustered at the tips of the stems, usually emerging with or shortly after the flowers, simple, lance-shaped with an entire margin, green. HABITAT: along streams, fens, and mountainous woodlands. COMMENTS: frequently attacked by a fungus called *Exobasidium rhododendri,* which transforms some leaves into fleshy fruit-like structures.

Early Azalea / *Rhododendron prinophyllum*

Calopogon, Grass Pink / *Calopogon tuberosus*

Indian-paintbrush / *Castilleja coccinea*

Moccasin Flower, Pink Lady's Slipper / *Cypripedium acaule*

Showy Orchis / *Galearis spectabilis*

Fringed Polygala, Gay-wings
•*Polygala paucifolia* Willd.
•Milkwort family Polygalaceae
FLOWERING SEASON: mid-May to early June. FLOWERS: rose-purple, 1 to 4, axial in the upper leaves, about ¾" (1.9 cm) long, appearing tubular with a fringed tip and two petal-like lateral sepals. PLANT: 4–7" (10–17.5 cm) tall; leaves alternate, simple, ovate with a pointed tip, margin entire, green. HABITAT: woodlands.

Comfrey
•*Symphytum officinale* L.
•Borage family Boraginaceae
FLOWERING SEASON: late May through July. FLOWERS: purple or yellow, many, in arched, typically terminal clusters, about ¾" (1.9 cm) long, tubular with 5 tiny lobes. PLANT: 2–3' (60–90 cm) tall; leaves alternate, simple, lance-shaped, hairy, margin entire, green. HABITAT: meadows and waste areas.

Cardinal Flower
•*Lobelia cardinalis* L.
•Bluebell family Campanulaceae
FLOWERING SEASON: mid-July through August. FLOWERS: scarlet, several to many in a showy, slender terminal cluster, about 1¼" (3.1 cm) long, tubular at the base, with 5 unequal spreading petal-like divisions. PLANT: 2–4½' (0.6–1.4 m) tall; leaves alternate, simple, lance-shaped, margin toothed, green. HABITAT: moist meadows, swamps, and edges of large bodies of water.

Common Burdock
•*Arctium minus* (Hill) Bernh.
•Aster family Asteraceae
FLOWERING SEASON: mid-July through August. FLOWERS: pink to lavender, flowerheads several to many in upper leaf axils, ½–¾" (1.3–1.9 cm) wide, rounded, surrounded by spiny green bracts. PLANT: 3–5' (1–1.5 m) tall; leaves alter-nate, simple, broadly ovate, heart-shaped near the base, margin entire, green. HABITAT: roadsides and waste areas.

Black Knapweed
•*Centaurea nigra* L.
•Aster family Asteraceae
FLOWERING SEASON: July–August. FLOWERS: rose-purple, flowerheads solitary to several, terminal, rounded, about 1" (2.5 cm) wide, base of flower somewhat spherical, covered with deeply fringed, black-tipped bracts. PLANT: 1–2' (30–60 cm) tall; leaves alternate and basal, sim-ple, oblong to lance-shaped, margin shal-lowly toothed to nearly entire, green. HABITAT: fields, roadsides and waste areas. COMMENTS: spotted knapweed, *Centaurea maculosa*, has many flower-heads and leaves with narrow, pinnately arranged lobes.

Saltmarsh Fleabane
•*Pluchea odorata* (L.) Cass
•Aster family Asteraceae
FLOWERING SEASON: August–September. FLOWERS: pinkish to purplish; flower-heads many, in small terminal and upper axial clusters about ¼" (6 mm) high, cylindrical, filamentous. PLANT: 2–3' (60–90 cm) tall; leaves alternate, simple, ovate to lance-shaped, margin toothed, green. HABITAT: coastal salt marshes. COMMENTS: the dried plant smells like mothballs.

Comfrey / *Symphytum officinale*

Common Burdock / *Arctium minus*

Fringed Polygala, Gaywings / *Polygala pauci-folia*

Black Knapweed / *Centaurea nigra*

Cardinal Flower / *Lobelia cardinalis*

Saltmarsh Fleabane / *Pluchea odorata*

Rose Pogonia, Snake-mouth
• *Pogonia ophioglossoides* (L.) Juss.
• Orchid family **Orchidaceae**
FLOWERING SEASON: late June through mid-July. **FLOWER**: pink, solitary, about 1¼" (3.1 cm) tall and wide, with 5 lance- to paddle-shaped petals and sepals above the lip; lip oblong with a fringed margin, pink with a central tuft of yellowish hair-like projections. **PLANT**: 8–15" (20–37.5 cm) tall; leaf usually solitary, on the lower stem, simple, oblong to obovate, margin entire, green. **HABITAT**: sphagnum fens, moist meadows, and swamps.

Small Purple Fringed Orchid
• *Platanthera psychodes* (L.) Lindl.
• Orchid family **Orchidaceae**
FLOWERING SEASON: late July through late August. **FLOWERS**: pale purple to lilac or occasionally white, 25 to 50 or more in a dense terminal cluster, ½–⅝" (1.3–1.6 cm) tall and wide, with 5 rounded petal-like parts and a heavily fringed 3-lobed lip with a long slender basal spur. **PLANT**: 1–3' (30–90 cm) tall; leaves alternate, simple, lance-shaped, margin entire, green. **HABITAT**: sunny moist meadows and fens. **COMMENTS**: the large purple fringed orchid, *Platanthera grandiflora*, has flowers that are about ¾" (1.9 cm) tall and wide in looser clusters, and are often darker in color. This shade-tolerant species begins blooming about one week earlier.

LEAVES ALTERNATE, COMPOUND OR DEEPLY DIVIDED

Red Columbine
• *Aquilegia canadensis* L.
• Crowfoot family **Ranunculaceae**
FLOWERING SEASON: mid-May through June. **FLOWERS**: scarlet, one to several, terminal, 1–2" (2.5–5 cm) long, with 5 tubular petals displaying yellow col- oration near the openings, nodding. **PLANT**: 1–2' (30–60 cm) tall; leaves alternate, compound with 3 to 9 leaflets; leaflets wedge-shaped and irregularly lobed, green. **HABITAT**: variable (e.g., rocky woodlands, wet cliffs, and roadsides), frequently near water.

Crown-vetch
• *Coronilla varia* L.
• Bean family **Fabaceae**
FLOWERING SEASON: June through early August. **FLOWERS**: bicolored, pink and white, many in dense, clover-like axial clusters about 1" (2.5 cm) wide; individual flowers about ⅜" (9 mm) long, narrowly pea-like. **PLANT**: prostrate or ascending, up to 2' (60 cm) tall; leaves alternate, pinnately compound with 11 to 25 leaflets; leaflets oblong, margins entire, green. **HABITAT**: roadsides and waste areas.

Beach-pea
• *Lathyrus japonicus* Willd.
• Bean family **Fabaceae**
FLOWERING SEASON: June into August. **FLOWERS**: bicolored, pinkish purple to violet and white, many, 6 to 10 in axial clusters, up to 1" (2.5 cm) long, pea-like. **PLANT**: vine, 1–2' (30–60 cm) long; leaves alternate, pinnately compound with 6 to 12 leaflets; leaflets oval, margins entire, green. **HABITAT**: ocean beaches, sometimes along large lakes.

Everlasting-pea
• *Lathyrus latifolius* L.
• Bean family **Fabaceae**
FLOWERING SEASON: late June to early August. **FLOWERS**: purplish pink, white or bluish, many, several in dense axial clusters, about 1" (2.5 cm) long, pea-like. **PLANT**: climbing vine, 2–5' (0.6–1.5 m) long; leaves alternate, compound with 2 leaflets and a winged stalk; leaflets oval, margins entire, green. **HABITAT**: roadsides, thickets, and waste areas.

Rose Pogonia, Snake-mouth / *Pogonia ophioglossoides*

Crown-vetch / *Coronilla varia*

Small Purple Fringed Orchid / *Platan-thera psychodes*

Beach-pea / *Lathyrus japonicus*

Red Columbine / *Aquilegia canadensis*

Everlasting-pea / *Lathyrus latifolius*

Red Clover
•*Trifolium pratense* L.
•Bean family **Fabaceae**
FLOWERING SEASON: late May into September. FLOWERS: pinkish red, many in 1" (2.5 cm) tall ovoid flowerheads, individual flowers about ½" (1.3 cm) long, narrow. PLANT: 6–24" (15–60 cm) tall; leaves alternate, compound with 3 leaflets; leaflets oval to oblong, margins nearly entire, green with pale green chevrons. HABITAT: fields and meadows. COMMENTS: *Trifolium incarnatum*, a slightly larger species with cylindrical crimson flowerheads, is occasionally planted along roadsides and fields.

Bull-thistle
•*Cirsium vulgare* (Savi) Tenore
•Aster family **Asteraceae**
FLOWERING SEASON: mid-July through August. FLOWERS: rose-purple, flowerheads several, terminal and upper axial, 1½–2" (3.8–5 cm) wide and high, filamentous, base of flowerhead urn-shaped and covered with numerous slender, spiny, yellow-tipped green bracts. PLANT: 2–5' (0.6–1.5 m) tall; leaves alternate, simple, deeply cleft, margin irregular, very sharply toothed and prickly, green. HABITAT: fields, roadsides, and waste areas.

Canada Thistle
•*Cirsium arvense* (L.) Scop.
•Aster family **Asteraceae**
FLOWERING SEASON: late June through July. FLOWERS: lavender to pale rose, flowerheads many, terminal and upper axial, about ¾" (1.9 cm) wide, filamentous, base of flowerhead somewhat spherical and covered with numerous slender spiny green bracts. PLANT: 1–3' (30–90 cm) tall; leaves alternate, simple, deeply cleft, margin irregular, very sharply toothed and prickly, green. HABITAT: fields and waste areas.

LEAVES OPPOSITE OR WHORLED, SIMPLE OR COMPOUND

Wild Basil
•*Clinopodium vulgare* L.
•Mint family **Lamiaceae**
FLOWERING SEASON: mid-June through September. FLOWERS: pink to purple, several to many in 1" (2.5 cm) wide terminal and axial clusters, about ⅜" (9 mm) long, tubular and 2-lipped; upper lip 3-lobed, lower lip 2-lobed. PLANT: 1–2' (30–60 cm) tall; leaves opposite, simple, ovate, margin wavy, green. HABITAT: woodlands.

Peppermint
•*Mentha aquatica* x *spicata* = *M*. x *piperita* L.
•Mint family **Lamiaceae**
FLOWERING SEASON: early August into September. FLOWERS: lavender, many in whorled, terminal, spike-like clusters, about ¼" (6 mm) long, tubular, 4-lobed. PLANT: 1–3' (30–90 cm) tall; leaves opposite on a square purplish stem, simple, lance-shaped, margin toothed, green HABITAT: moist soils. COMMENTS: the highly fragrant leaves are the source of the well-known herbal tea.

Peppermint / *Mentha aquatica* x *spicata*

Wild Basil / *Clinopodium vulgare*

Red Clover / *Trifolium pratense*

Trifolium incarnatum

Canada Thistle / *Cirsium arvense*

Bull-thistle / *Cirsium vulgare*

Bee-balm

- *Monarda didyma* L.
- Mint family **Lamiaceae**

FLOWERING SEASON: July–August. FLOW-ERS: scarlet, many in a rounded terminal cluster, about 1¾" (4.4 cm) long, tubular with 2 elongated lips; upper lip 2-lobed; lower lip 3-lobed. PLANT: 2–3' (60–90 cm) tall; leaves opposite on a square stem, simple, broadly lance-shaped, margin toothed, green. HABITAT: moist, often shaded, soils. COMMENTS: a domesticated form is commonly cultivated and is frequently visited by hummingbirds.

Bergamot

- *Monarda fistulosa* L.
- Mint family **Lamiaceae**

FLOWERING SEASON: mid-July through August. FLOWERS: lavender, many, in one or more rounded terminal clusters, about 1¼" (3.1 cm) long, tubular with 2 elongated lips; upper lip 2-lobed, lower lip 3-lobed. PLANT: 2–3' (60–90 cm) tall; leaves opposite on a square stem, simple, lance-shaped to ovate with a pointed tip, margin toothed, green. HABITAT: dry meadows.

Purple Dead-nettle

- *Lamium purpureum* L.
- Mint family **Lamiaceae**

FLOWERING SEASON: May. FLOWERS: purple-red, several, in axillary and terminal clusters, up to ½" (1.3 cm) long, tubular with 2 lips; upper lip 2-lobed and hairy; lower lip 3-lobed. PLANT: 6–18" (15–45 cm) tall; leaves opposite on a square stem, simple, ovate on the upper portion, heart-shaped at the base, margin bluntly toothed, green. HABITAT: roadsides and waste areas.

Wild Thyme

- *Thymus pulegioides* L.
- Mint family **Lamiaceae**

FLOWERING SEASON: mid-July to early September. FLOWERS: purple, many in rounded terminal and axial clusters, tiny, tubular with 2 lips; upper lip entire; lower lip 3-lobed. PLANT: prostrate and creeping, 4–12" (10–30 cm) long; leaves tiny, opposite on a square stem, simple, oblong, margin entire, green. HABITAT: roadsides and meadows. COMMENTS: thyme makes an excellent culinary seasoning.

Trumpet-creeper

- *Campsis radicans* (L.) Seem. ex Bureau
- Bignonia family **Bignoniaceae**

FLOWERING SEASON: July–August. FLOWERS: scarlet to reddish orange, many, in terminal clusters of 2 to 9, about 2½" (6.3 cm) long, tubular with 5 shallow, rounded lobes. PLANT: woody vine, 20–40' (6–12 m) long; leaves opposite, pinnately compound with 7 to 11 leaflets; leaflets broadly lance-shaped, margins toothed, green. HABITAT: woodlands and thickets.

Trumpet Honeysuckle

- *Lonicera sempervirens* L.
- Honeysuckle family **Caprifoliaceae**

FLOWERING SEASON: June–July. FLOWERS: scarlet, several whorled in a terminal spike, 1–1½" (2.5–3.8 cm) long, tubular with 5 small petal-like lobes. PLANT: vine-like; leaves opposite, upper pairs joined and perfoliate, simple, oval, margin entire, green. HABITAT: woodlots, hedgerows, and edges of woodlands.

Bergamot / *Monarda fistulosa*

Wild Thyme / *Thymus pulegioides*

Bee-balm / *Monarda didyma*

Purple Dead-nettle / *Lamium pur-
pureum*

Trumpet-creeper / *Campsis radicans*

Trumpet Honeysuckle / *Lonicera sempervirens*

Glaucous Honeysuckle
•*Lonicera dioica* L.
•Honeysuckle family **Caprifoliaceae**
FLOWERING SEASON: June. **FLOWERS:** yellowish, later darkening to reddish purple, 2 to 4 or more on a terminal cluster, about 1" (2.5 cm) long, corolla tubular with 5 flaring lobes. **PLANT:** vine-like, up to 9' (2.7 m) long, leaves opposite, upper pair joined and perfoliate, simple, oval, margin entire, green. **HABITAT:** woodlands and thickets. **COMMENTS:** hairy honeysuckle, *Lonicera hirsuta*, has orange-yellow flowers and leaves with minutely hairy margins.

Teasel
•*Dipsacus fullonum* L.
•Teasel family **Dipsacaceae**
FLOWERING SEASON: August. **FLOWERS:** lavender, many, on oval to cylindrical terminal flowerheads; individual flowers about ½" (1.3 cm) long, tubular with 4 tiny rounded lobes. **PLANT:** 3–6' (0.9–1.8 m) tall; leaves opposite on a spiny stem, simple, oblong to lance-shaped, prickly on the lower central vein, margin entire to bluntly toothed, green. **HABITAT:** fields and waste areas.

Joe-pye-weed, Red Boneset
•*Eupatorium purpureum* L.
•Aster family **Asteraceae**
FLOWERING SEASON: August to late September. **FLOWERS:** pink to purplish pink, flowerheads many, in dense terminal clusters, about $^{5}/_{16}$" (8 mm) wide, filamentous. **PLANT:** 3–10' (0.9–3 m) tall; leaves in whorls of 3 to 6, simple, lance-shaped, margin toothed, green; stem mostly green. **HABITAT:** moist soil in roadsides, fields, swamps, and woodland edges. **COMMENTS:** spotted joe-pye-weed, *Eupatorium maculatum*, is a very similar species with flat-topped flower clusters and a purple or purple-spotted stem. Ironweed, *Veronia noveboracensis*, found in southeastern New York, has open, loose flower clusters and alternate leaves.

Teasel / *Dipsacus fullonum*

Joe-pye-weed, Red Boneset / *Eupatorium pur-pureum*

Glaucous Honeysuckle / *Lonicera dioica*

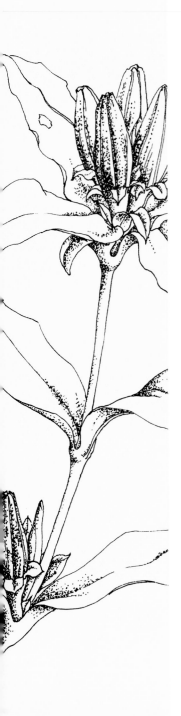

PART THREE

YELLOW TO ORANGE FLOWERS

❧

FLOWERS SYMMETRICAL, WITH 3 PETALS OR PETAL-LIKE PARTS

LEAVES BASAL, SIMPLE

Northern Yellow-eyed Grass

• *Xyris montana* Ries
• Yellow-eyed Grass family Xyridaceae

FLOWERING SEASON: July. FLOWERS: yellow, one to few, terminal from a small cone-like head on a very slender stem, about ¼" (6 mm) wide, with 3 rounded, petal-like parts. PLANT: 2–12" (5–30 cm) tall; leaves mostly basal, simple, long and very narrow, margin entire, green. HABITAT: fens and bogs.

Yellow Iris, Yellow Flag

• *Iris pseudacorus* L.
• Iris family Iridaceae

FLOWERING SEASON: June through early July. FLOWERS: yellow, several, terminal on an upright stem, about 3¼" (8.1 cm) wide, perianth, 6-parted, outer 3 parts obovate with down-turned tips, inner 3 parts smaller, oblong and nearly erect. PLANT: 1½–3' (45–90 cm) tall; leaves basal, simple, long and narrow, margin entire, bluish green. HABITAT: marshes, wet meadows, and along bodies of water.

FLOWERS SYMMETRICAL, WITH 4 PETALS OR PETAL-LIKE PARTS

LEAVES BASAL, COMPOUND

Wintercress

• *Barbarea vulgaris* R. Br. ex Ait.
• Mustard family Brassicaceae

FLOWERING SEASON: mid-May to mid-June. FLOWERS: yellow, several to many in axial and terminal clusters, about 5/16" (8 mm) wide, cross-shaped, with 4 oval petals. PLANT: 1–2' (30–60 cm) tall; leaves alternate and basal, upper leaves usually with a few large teeth, basal leaves with a large, oval, toothless terminal division and 1 to 4 pairs of much smaller lobes along the stalk, green; seed pods about 1" (2.5 cm) long, slender, somewhat spreading. HABITAT: fields and waste areas. COMMENTS: black mustard, *Brassica nigra*, which blooms immediately after wintercress, is a much taller plant with paler yellow flowers and slender ½" (1.3 cm) long seed pods that clasp the stem. Charlock, *Sinapis arvensis*, is 1–2' (30–60 cm) tall and has 5/8" (1.6 cm) long seed pods that are constricted around the circular seeds.

LEAVES ALTERNATE, SIMPLE

Witch-hazel

• *Hamamelis virginiana* L.
• Witch-hazel family Hamamelidaceae

FLOWERING SEASON: October. FLOWERS: yellow, many, in axillary clusters of 2 to several, about 1" (2.5 cm) wide, with 4 long and very narrow petals. PLANT: shrub, 5–25' (1.5–7.5 m) tall; leaves alternate, simple, oval with an asymmetrical base, margin with large rounded teeth, green. HABITAT: wooded swamps, moist woodlands.

Evening Primrose

• *Oenothera biennis* L.
• Evening Primrose family Onagraceae

FLOWERING SEASON: July–September. FLOWERS: yellow, several in a terminal cluster, about 1–2" (2.5–5 cm) wide, with 4 rounded, slightly notched petals. PLANT: 1–9' (0.3–2.7 m) tall; leaves alternate, simple, lance-shaped, margin slightly wavy, green. HABITAT: in dry, sunny soils such as roadsides and fields. COMMENTS: flowers open in early evening and remain open through the following morning.

Northern Yellow-eyed Grass / *Xyris montana*

Wintercress / *Barbarea vulgaris*

Witch-hazel / *Hamamelis virginiana*

Yellow Iris, Yellow Flag / *Iris pseudacorus*

Evening Primrose / *Oenothera biennis*

LEAVES ALTERNATE, COMPOUND OR DEEPLY DIVIDED

Celandine
- *Chelidonium majus* L.
- Poppy family **Papaveraceae**

FLOWERING SEASON: mid-May through June. FLOWERS: yellow, few to several, in loose terminal clusters, about ⅝" (1.6 cm) wide, with 4 rounded petals. PLANT: 1–2' (30–60 cm) tall; leaves alternate, appearing pinnately compound, margin unevenly bluntly toothed, green. HABITAT: moist places and woodlands. COMMENTS: the damaged plant exudes bright yellow sap.

Creeping Yellow-cress
- *Rorippa sylvestris* (L.) Besser
- Mustard family **Brassicaceae**

FLOWERING SEASON: June to mid-August. FLOWERS: yellow, several to many, in slender terminal clusters, about ¼" (6 mm) wide, with 4 rounded petals. PLANT: often somewhat prostrate, 6–12" (15–30 cm) tall; leaves alternate, pinnately divided into 5 to 11 oblong lobes, margin coarsely toothed, green; seed pods narrow, ⁵⁄₁₆–½" (8–13 mm) long, long-stalked. HABITAT: waste areas, edges of lakes and rivers.

LEAVES OPPOSITE OR WHORLED, SIMPLE

Yellow Bedstraw
- *Galium verum* L.
- Madder family **Rubiaceae**

FLOWERING SEASON: June–July. FLOWERS: yellow, many, in densely flowered terminal and axial clusters, tiny, corolla with 4 sharply pointed, petal-like lobes. PLANT: 6–30" (15–75 cm) tall; leaves in whorls of 6 to 8, simple, very narrow, margin entire, green. HABITAT: fields and waste areas.

FLOWERS SYMMETRICAL, WITH 5 PETALS OR PETAL-LIKE PARTS

LEAVES BASAL, SIMPLE

Marsh Marigold, American Cowslip
- *Caltha palustris* L.
- Crowfoot family **Ranunculaceae**

FLOWERING SEASON: late April through May. FLOWERS: yellow, several in a showy terminal cluster, about 1¼" (3.1 cm) wide, with 5 large rounded petal-like sepals. PLANT: 1–2' (30–60 cm) tall; leaves mostly basal, simple, heart- to kidney-shaped with a broadly rounded tip, margin entire to slightly scalloped, green. HABITAT: swamps and wet meadows.

LEAVES BASAL, COMPOUND

Barren Strawberry, False Strawberry
- *Waldsteinia fragarioides* (Michx.) Tratt.
- Rose family **Rosaceae**

FLOWERING SEASON: late April through May. FLOWERS: yellow, several in a loose terminal cluster, about ⁵⁄₁₆" (8 mm) wide, with 5 rounded petals. PLANT: creeping, 3–7" (7.5–17.5 cm) tall; leaves alternate or mostly basal, compound with 3 leaflets; leaflets obovate, margins toothed, green. HABITAT: woodlands and shaded hillsides.

LEAVES ALTERNATE, SIMPLE

Purslane
- *Portulaca oleracea* L.
- Purslane family **Portulacaceae**

FLOWERING SEASON: July–September. FLOWERS: yellow, several, individual flowers found in the center of axial leaf clusters, up to ¼" (6 mm) wide, with 5 broad petals. PLANT: prostrate; leaves alternate or clustered at the end of 4–10" (10–25 cm) long purple stems, simple, obovate, thick and fleshy, margin entire, green. HABITAT: fields and waste areas.

Celandine / *Chelidonium majus*

Creeping Yellow-cress / *Rorippa sylvestris*

Yellow Bedstraw / *Galium verum*

Marsh Marigold, American Cowslip / *Caltha palustris*

Purslane / *Portulaca oleracea*

Barren Strawberry, False Strawberry / *Waldsteinia fragarioides*

Velvet-leaf

• *Abutilon theophrasti* Medic.
• Mallow family **Malvaceae**
FLOWERING SEASON: mid-August to late September. FLOWERS: yellow to orange-yellow, 1 to 3 in the upper axils, about ¾" (1.9 cm) wide, with 5 rounded petals. PLANT: about 3–6' (0.9–1.8 m) tall; leaves alternate, simple, heart-shaped, large, margin entire, green. HABITAT: waste areas and fields, especially with recently disturbed soil. COMMENTS: a nuisance plant of farmers' fields.

Mossy Stonecrop

• *Sedum acre* L.
• Sedum family **Crassulaceae**
FLOWERING SEASON: mid-June to mid-July. FLOWERS: bright yellow, several scattered along spreading stems, about ⅜" (9 mm) wide, with 4 to 5 lance-shaped petals. PLANT: creeping and spreading, 1–3" (2.5–7.5 cm) tall; leaves alternate, simple, ovate and appearing scale-like, thick and fleshy, margin entire, light green. HABITAT: on rocks and rocky soil, often wet areas.

Wild Black Currant

• *Ribes americanum* Mill.
• Currant family **Grossulariaceae**
FLOWERING SEASON: May. FLOWERS: greenish yellow, many, in drooping axial clusters of about 10, about ⁵⁄₁₆" (8 mm) long, with 5 petals. PLANT: shrub, 3–4' (0.9–1.2 m) tall; leaves alternate and often clustered, simple, broadly maple-like with 3 to 5 lobes, margins toothed, green; fruit a drooping cluster of smooth ¼" (6 mm) black berries. HABITAT: moist woodlands and swamps. COMMENTS: wild gooseberry, *R. cynos-bati*, is a similar woodland shrub with bell-shaped flowers in clusters of 1 to 3 and ⁵⁄₁₆–½" (8–13 mm) prickle-skinned fruit.

Butterfly-weed

• *Asclepias tuberosa* L.
• Milkweed family **Asclepiadaceae**
FLOWERING SEASON: mid-July through August. FLOWERS: orange, many in rounded terminal clusters, about ¼" (6 mm) wide, with 5 deeply recurved petals and a 5-pointed crown-like center. PLANT: 1–2' (30–60 cm) tall; leaves alternate, simple, narrowly oblong, margin entire, green. HABITAT: dry, often sandy soils.

Clammy Ground-cherry

• *Physalis heterophylla* Nees
• Nightshade family **Solanaceae**
FLOWERING SEASON: July–September. FLOWERS: greenish yellow to yellowish with a brownish to purplish center, several, scattered throughout the plant in axils, about ¾" (1.9 cm) wide, corolla broadly bell-shaped with 5 petal-like lobes, nodding. PLANT: about 1½–3' (45–90 cm) tall; leaves alternate along hairy branching stems, simple, obovate to broadly heart-shaped, margin toothed, green; fruit an edible spherical berry surrounded by a papery lantern-like husk. HABITAT: roadsides, waste areas, and previously cultivated fields. COMMENTS: numerous look-alike species occur.

LEAVES ALTERNATE, COMPOUND OR DEEPLY DIVIDED

Agrimony

• *Agrimonia striata* Michx.
• Rose family **Rosaceae**
FLOWERING SEASON: August into September. FLOWERS: yellow, several to many in slender (usually terminal) clusters, about ³⁄₁₆" (5 mm) wide, with 5 rounded petals. PLANT: 1–5' (0.3–1.5 m) tall; leaves alternate, pinnately compound typically with 5 large leaflets and smaller ones in between; large leaflets oblong to obovate, coarsely toothed,

Wild Black Currant / *Ribes americanum*

Mossy Stonecrop / *Sedum acre*

Velvet-leaf / *Abutilon theophrasti*

Butterfly-weed / *Asclepias tuberosa*

Agrimony / *Agrimonia striata*

Clammy Ground-cherry / *Physalis heterophylla*

green; smaller leaflets lance-shaped, margins entire, green. HABITAT: dry woodlands.

Swamp Buttercup
•*Ranunculus hispidus* Michx.
•Crowfoot family **Ranunculaceae**
FLOWERING SEASON: late April to late May. FLOWERS: bright yellow, several, terminal, 1" (2.5 cm) or more wide, with 5 ovate petals. PLANT: 1–3' (30–90 cm) tall; leaves alternate, divided into 3 segments, leaflets distinctly stalked, margins sharply and unevenly toothed, green. HABITAT: swamps and moist low ground.

Creeping Buttercup
•*Ranunculus repens* L.
•Crowfoot family **Ranunculaceae**
FLOWERING SEASON: May–June. FLOWERS: bright yellow, several, terminal, nearly 1" (2.5 cm) wide, with 5 ovate petals. PLANT: creeping, usually less than 1' (30 cm) tall; leaves alternate, divided into 3 segments, terminal segment stalked, lateral segments stalkless, margins unevenly toothed, green with greenish white blotches. HABITAT: fields, roadsides, and waste areas.

Common Cinquefoil
•*Potentilla simplex* Michx.
•Rose family **Rosaceae**
FLOWERING SEASON: July. FLOWERS: yellow, few, terminal or in axils, ¼–½" (6–13 mm) wide, with 5 rounded petals. PLANT: trailing, stem 3–24" (7.5–60 cm) long; leaves alternate, palmately compound with 5 leaflets; leaflets oblong to lance-shaped, margins toothed, green; stem hairy. HABITAT: fields, waste areas, and open woods.

Sulfur Cinquefoil, Five-fingers
•*Potentilla recta* L.
•Rose family **Rosaceae**
FLOWERING SEASON: mid-June to mid-August. FLOWERS: sulphur-yellow with an orange center, several to many in a loose terminal cluster, ½–¾" (1.3–1.9 cm) wide, with 5 notched petals. PLANT: 1–2' (30–60 cm) tall; leaves alternate, palmately divided with 5 to 7 lobes; margin coarsely toothed, somewhat pubescent, green; stem hairy. HABITAT: fields and waste areas.

Rough Cinquefoil
•*Potentilla norvegica* L.
•Rose family **Rosaceae**
FLOWERING SEASON: July. FLOWERS: yellow, several, terminal, up to ½" (1.3 cm) wide, with 5 rounded petals. PLANT: 6–30" (15–75 cm) tall; leaves alternate, 3-lobed, leaflets ovate to lance-shaped, margins toothed, green; stem roughened with short, stiff hairs. HABITAT: cultivated fields, waste areas, and roadsides.

Shrubby Cinquefoil
•*Potentilla fruticosa* L.
•Rose family **Rosaceae**
FLOWERING SEASON : late June through July. FLOWERS: bright yellow, solitary to several, terminal, ¾–1¼" (1.9–3.1 cm) wide, with 5 rounded petals. PLANT: shrub, 6–48" (15–120 cm) tall; leaves alternate, pinnately compound with 5 to 7 leaflets; leaflets oblong to lance-shaped, silky-pubescent, margins entire or slightly toothed, green. HABITAT: swamps and moist rocky places.

Swamp Buttercup / *Ranunculus hispidus*

Creeping Buttercup / *Ranunculus repens*

Common Cinquefoil / *Potentilla simplex*

Sulfur Cinquefoil, Five-fingers / *Potentilla recta*

Rough Cinquefoil / *Potentilla norvegica*

Shrubby Cinquefoil / *Potentilla fruticosa*

Wild Senna
- *Senna hebecarpa* (Fern.) Irwin & Barneby
- Mimosa family **Mimosaceae**

FLOWERING SEASON: August. FLOWERS: yellow with brown markings, many, in upper axial clusters, ½–¾" (1.3–1.9 cm) wide, with 5 rounded petals. PLANT: 3–8' (1–2.4 m) tall; leaves alternate, pinnately compound with 12 to 20 leaflets; leaflets oblong, margins entire, green. HABITAT: swamps and moist meadows.

Yellow Wood-sorrel, Sour Grass
- *Oxalis stricta* L.
- Oxalis family **Oxalidaceae**

FLOWERING SEASON: mid-May–August. FLOWERS: yellow, solitary to several in leaf axils, about ½" (1.3 cm) wide, with 5 nearly round petals. PLANT: 4–12" (10–30 cm) tall; leaves alternate, compound with 3 leaflets; leaflets heart-shaped, margins entire, green, sour-tasting. HABITAT: roadsides, waste areas, fields, and open woodlands.

Wild Parsnip
- *Pastinaca sativa* L.
- Carrot family **Apiaceae**

FLOWERING SEASON: mid-June to mid-July. FLOWERS: yellow, many, in rounded, flat-topped terminal clusters 2–6" (5–15 cm) wide; individual flowers tiny, with 5 petals. PLANT: 2–5' (0.6–1.5 m) tall; leaves alternate, pinnately compound; leaflets ovate, lobed, margin toothed, green. HABITAT: roadsides, fields, and waste areas.

Yellow Pimpernel
- *Taenidia integerrima* (L.) Drude
- Carrot family **Apiaceae**

FLOWERING SEASON: late May into June. FLOWERS: yellow, many in loose, spherical terminal clusters 3–5" (7.5–12.5 cm) wide; individual flowers tiny, with 5 petals. PLANT: 1–3' (30–90 cm) tall; leaves alternate, compound with 3 divisions typically having 7 to 21 leaflets; leaflets ovate to oval, margins entire, green. HABITAT: rocky, usually moist, soil.

LEAVES OPPOSITE, SIMPLE

Canadian St. John's-wort
- *Hypericum canadense* L.
- Mangosteen family **Clusiaceae**

FLOWERING SEASON: July–August. FLOWERS: yellow, several, in loosely flowered terminal clusters, about ¼" (6 mm) wide, with 5 rounded petals. PLANT: 6–20" (15–50 cm) tall; leaves opposite, simple, very narrow, margin entire, green. HABITAT: wet, sandy soil.

Swamp-candles
- *Lysimachia terrestris* (L.) BSP.
- Primrose family **Primulaceae**

FLOWERING SEASON: late June through July. FLOWERS: yellow with purple markings surrounding the center, many in a tall, slender terminal cluster, about ⅜" (9 mm) wide with 5 narrow petal-like lobes. PLANT: 8–24" (20–60 cm) tall; leaves mostly opposite, simple, lance-shaped, margin entire, green. HABITAT: swamps and moist areas.

Wild Parsnip / *Pastinaca sativa*

Canadian St. John's-wort / *Hypericum canadense*

Yellow Pimpernel / *Taenidia integerrima*

Yellow Wood-sorrel, Sour Grass / *Oxalis stricta*

Swamp-candles / *Lysimachia terrestris*

Wild Senna / *Senna hebecarpa*

Fringed Loosestrife
•*Lysimachia ciliata* L.
•Primrose family **Primulaceae**
FLOWERING SEASON: mid-July to mid-August. FLOWERS: yellow, several in small axial groups, about ¾" (1.9 cm) wide, with 5 rounded, fringed-tipped, petal-like lobes. PLANT: 1–4' (0.3–1.2 m) tall; leaves opposite or whorled, simple, broadly lance-shaped, margin entire, green. HABITAT: moist meadows and thickets.

Moneywort, Creeping-Charlie
•*Lysimachia nummularia* L.
•Primrose family **Primulaceae**
FLOWERING SEASON: mid-June to mid-July. FLOWERS: yellow, several, in axial pairs, up to 1" (2.5 cm) wide, with 5 rounded, petal-like lobes. PLANT: prostrate with stems up to 2' (60 cm) long; leaves opposite, simple, nearly round, margin entire, green. HABITAT: moist fields and open woodlands.

Golden Currant
•*Ribes aureum* Pursh var. *villosum* DC.
•Currant family **Grossulariaceae**
FLOWERING SEASON: mid-May to mid-June. FLOWERS: yellow, many, scattered along the branches, about ¾" (1.9 cm) long, tubular with 5 oblong, spreading, petal-like lobes; spicy fragrance. PLANT: shrub, 3–5' (0.9–1.5 m) tall; leaves opposite or clustered, simple, triangular and usually 3-lobed; lobes few-toothed or entire, green. HABITAT: along streams, canals, and other waterways.

FLOWERS SYMMETRICAL, WITH 6 PETALS OR PETAL-LIKE PARTS

AQUATIC, LEAVES FLOATING OR JUST ABOVE WATER

Yellow Pond-lily, Spatterdock
•*Nuphar luteum* (L.) Sibth. and Smith
•Waterlily family **Nymphaeaceae**
FLOWERING SEASON: mid-June through August. FLOWERS: yellow, solitary, terminal, 1½–3½" (4–9 cm) wide, with usually 6 oblong petal-like sepals. PLANT: leaves up to 1' (30 cm) long, usually floating, simple, ovate with a deeply heart-shaped base, margin entire, green. HABITAT: aquatic, including ponds, lakes, and slowly moving streams. COMMENTS: some authorities now consider this a complex of several species.

LEAVES BASAL, SIMPLE

Lemon-lily, Yellow Daylily
•*Hemerocallis lilioasphodelus* L.
•Lily family **Liliaceae**
FLOWERING SEASON: mid-May through June. FLOWERS: yellow, several on a tall stem with only 1 to 3 blooming at a time, about 4" (10 cm) long, large and showy, trumpet-shaped, perianth with 6 flaring and somewhat recurved parts. PLANT: 3–4' (0.9–1.2 m) tall; leaves many, basal, simple, long and narrow, margin entire, green. HABITAT: fields, roadsides. COMMENTS: unlike the orange daylily, *H. fulva*, the lemon lily produces seeds.

Orange Daylily
•*Hemerocallis fulva* (L.) L.
•Lily family **Liliaceae**
FLOWERING SEASON: mid-June through July. FLOWERS: orange, 6 to 15 on a tall stem with only 1 to 3 blooming at a time, about 4–5" (10–12.5 cm) long, large and showy, trumpet-shaped, perianth with 6 flaring and recurved parts. PLANT: 3–6' (0.9–1.8 m) tall; leaves many, basal, simple, long and narrow, margin entire, green. HABITAT: fields, roadsides. COMMENTS: flowers last only one day, hence the common name daylily.

Moneywort, Creeping-Charlie / *Lysimachia nummularia*

Fringed Loosestrife / *Lysimachia ciliata*

Golden Currant / *Ribes aureum*

Yellow Pond-lily, Spatterdock / *Nuphar luteum*

Orange Daylily / *Hemerocallis fulva*

Lemon-lily, Yellow Daylily / *Hemerocallis lilioasphodelus*

Troutlily, Dog-tooth Violet
•*Erythronium americanum* Ker
•Lily family **Liliaceae**

FLOWERING SEASON: late April to mid-May. FLOWER: yellow, solitary, terminal, about 1¼" (3.1 cm) long, perianth with 6 lance-shaped spreading to somewhat recurved parts. PLANT: 6–12" (15–30 cm) tall; leaves 2, basal, simple, lance-shaped, margin entire, fleshy, green, often with purplish or brownish mottling. HABITAT: woodlands. COMMENTS: the white troutlily, *Erythronium albidum*, which has white, deeply recurved petals, is occasionally found in New York State.

Clintonia, Woodlily
•*Clintonia borealis* (Ait.) Raf.
•Lily family **Liliaceae**

FLOWERING SEASON: late May through June. FLOWERS: yellow to greenish yellow, 3 to 6 in a terminal cluster, about ¾" (1.9 cm) long, perianth with 6 long, narrow, petal-like parts, usually drooping. PLANT: 6–15" (15–37.5 cm) tall; leaves usually 3, basal, simple, oval, margin entire, green. HABITAT: woodlands. COMMENTS: the white woodlily, *Clintonia umbellulata*, which has white flowers and hairy leaf margins, has been recorded in western New York.

LEAVES ALTERNATE, SIMPLE

Tiger Lily
•*Lilium lancifolium* Thunb.
•Lily family **Liliaceae**

FLOWERING SEASON: mid-July to mid-August. FLOWERS: orange-red, conspicuously purple-spotted inside, 5 to 25 flowers in a terminal cluster, about 3¼" (8.1 cm) wide, perianth with 6 large, spreading, and deeply recurved petal-like parts, stamens fully protruding, nodding. PLANT: 2–5' (0.6–1.5 m) tall; leaves alternate, simple, lance-shaped, margin entire, green; blackish bulblets in the upper axils. HABITAT: fields, hedgerows, and roadsides.

Wild-oats
•*Uvularia sessilifolia* L.
•Lily family **Liliaceae**

FLOWERING SEASON: mid- to late May. FLOWERS: greenish yellow, solitary, axial, about 1" (2.5 cm) long, perianth with 6 long, narrow, petal-like parts, nodding. PLANT: 10–12" (25–30 cm) tall; leaves alternate along a forking stem, simple, lance-shaped, margin entire, green. HABITAT: woodlands.

Bellwort
•*Uvularia grandiflora* Sm.
•Lily family **Liliaceae**

FLOWERING SEASON: mid-April to mid-May. FLOWER: yellow, usually solitary and terminal, about 1¼" (3.1 cm) long, perianth with 6 long, narrow, petal-like parts, smooth or slightly granular within, nodding. PLANT: 6–20" (15–50 cm) tall; leaves alternate on a forking stem, simple, oblong to oval, penetrated by the stem, margin entire, lower surface pubescent during flowering season, green. HABITAT: woodlands.

LEAVES ALTERNATE, COMPOUND OR DEEPLY LOBED

Globeflower
•*Trollius laxus* Salisb.
•Crowfoot family **Ranunculaceae**

FLOWERING SEASON: mid-April into May. FLOWER: pale greenish yellow, usually solitary, terminal, about 1½" (3.8 cm) wide, with 5 to 7 oval petal-like sepals. PLANT: 6–18" (15–45 cm) tall; leaves alternate, compound with 5 to 7 deeply cut lobes, lower leaves long-stalked, margins sharply and deeply toothed, green. HABITAT: swamps and wet meadows. COMMENTS: *protected. Threatened. Do not disturb.*

Troutlily, Dog-tooth Violet / *Erythronium americanum*

Tiger Lily / *Lilium lancifolium*

Globeflower / *Trollius laxus*

Clintonia, Woodlily / *Clintonia borealis*

Bellwort / *Uvularia grandiflora*

Wild-oats / *Uvularia sessilifolia*

LEAVES OPPOSITE OR WHORLED, SIMPLE

Common Barberry
- *Berberis vulgaris* L.
- Barberry family **Berberidaceae**

FLOWERING SEASON: mid-May to mid-June. **FLOWERS:** yellow, several to many in pendant, slender axial clusters, about ⁵⁄₁₆" (8 mm) wide, with 6 rounded petals. **PLANT:** shrub, 6–8' (1.8–2 4 m) tall; leaves opposite or whorled, simple, paddle-shaped, margin sharply toothed, green. **HABITAT:** thickets, pastures and hedgerows. **COMMENTS:** the scarlet oblong berries are pleasantly acidic.

Indian Cucumber-root
- *Medeola virginiana* L.
- Lily family **Liliaceae**

FLOWERING SEASON: June to early July. **FLOWERS:** greenish yellow, 2 to 9 in a drooping terminal cluster, about ¾" (1.9 cm) wide, perianth with 6 petal-like parts. **PLANT:** 1–2½' (30–75 cm) tall; leaves in 2 whorls; leaves of lower whorl large and about 6 in number, leaves of upper whorl smaller, fewer, terminal; simple, lance-shaped, margin entire, green. **HABITAT:** woodlands.

Woodlily
- *Lilium philadelphicum* L.
- Lily family **Liliaceae**

FLOWERING SEASON: late June to early July. **FLOWER:** reddish orange, purple-spotted inside, usually solitary or sometimes 2, terminal, about 3½" (8.8 cm) wide, perianth with 6 spreading, petal-like parts, flower facing upwards. **PLANT:** 1–3' (30–90 cm) tall; leaves whorled, simple, lance-shaped, margin entire, green. **HABITAT:** woods and thickets.

Canada Lily
- *Lilium canadense* L.
- Lily family **Liliaceae**

FLOWERING SEASON: late June to mid-July. **FLOWERS:** yellow, occasionally red, with numerous spots inside, 1 to 16 in showy terminal clusters, about 3¾" (9.4 cm) wide, perianth with 6 large, spreading and somewhat recurved petal-like parts, thickened tips of stamens protruding from flowers, nodding. **PLANT:** 2–5' (0.6–1.5 m) tall; leaves whorled, simple, lance-shaped, margin entire, green. **HABITAT:** swamps, moist meadows, and fields.

Turk's-cap Lily
- *Lilium superbum* L.
- Lily family **Liliaceae**

FLOWERING SEASON: July. **FLOWERS:** orange, orange-yellow or occasionally red, purple-spotted inside, 3 to 40 in showy terminal clusters, about 3" (7.5 cm) wide, perianth with 6 large, spreading, and deeply recurved petal-like parts, nearly all of the stamens protruding from flowers, nodding. **PLANT:** 3–8' (0.9–2.4 m) tall; leaves whorled, simple, lance-shaped, margin entire, green. **HABITAT:** meadows and open moist areas.

FLOWERS SYMMETRICAL, WITH 7 OR MORE PETALS OR PETAL-LIKE PARTS

LACKING TYPICAL LEAVES

Prickly Pear
- *Opuntia humifusa* (Raf.) Raf.
- Cactus family **Cactaceae**

FLOWERING SEASON: July. **FLOWERS:** yellow, several, arising from pads, 2½–3½" (6.3–8.8 cm) wide, with numerous broad petals. **PLANT:** usually prostrate; pads obovate to oval, thick and fleshy, covered with clusters of needle-like spines, green. **HABITAT:** in sandy soil, in New York limited to the southeastern portion of the state. **COMMENTS:** New York's only cactus species.

Common Barberry / *Berberis vulgaris*

Indian Cucumber-root / *Medeola virginiana*

Woodlily / *Lilium philadelphicum*

Canada Lily / *Lilium canadense*

Turk's-cap Lily / *Lilium superbum*

Prickly Pear / *Opuntia humifusa*

AQUATIC, LEAVES SUSPENDED ABOVE WATER

Yellow Lotus
•*Nelumbo lutea* (Willd.) Pers.
•Lotus family **Nelumbonaceae**
FLOWERING SEASON: mid-July to mid-August. FLOWER: pale yellow, solitary, rising above the water on a single stalk, 4–10" (10–25 cm) wide, with many obovate petals. PLANT: leaves 1–2' (30–60 cm) wide, usually held above water or occasionally floating, simple, nearly round and somewhat funnel-shaped, margin entire, green. HABITAT: aquatic (lakes and slowly moving rivers). COMMENTS: the dried seed-head, which resembles an old-fashioned shower head, is commonly used in dried flower arrangements.

LEAVES BASAL, SIMPLE

Dandelion
•*Taraxacum officinale* Weber ex Wiggers
•Aster family **Asteraceae**
FLOWERING SEASON: late April to early June; a few into fall. FLOWERS: yellow; flowerheads 1 to few on terminal stalks, about 1½" (3.8 cm) wide, rimmed with many oblong, minutely 5-toothed, petal-like rays. PLANT: 2–18" (5–45 cm) tall; leaves basal, simple, oblong to paddle-shaped, margin unevenly and coarsely toothed, green. HABITAT: fields, lawns, and waste areas.

Coltsfoot
•*Tussilago farfara* L.
•Aster family **Asteraceae**
FLOWERING SEASON: April–May. FLOWERS: yellow; flowerheads few, each terminal on an individual scaly 3–18" (7.5–45 cm) tall stem, about 1" (2.5 cm) wide, rimmed with many narrow, petal-like rays, blooming before the leaves emerge. LEAVES: basal, simple, nearly round with very shallow angularly-sided lobes, margin toothed, green, pubescent underneath. HABITAT: moist soil, meadows, and roadsides.

Rattlesnake-weed
•*Hieracium venosum* L.
•Aster family **Asteraceae**
FLOWERING SEASON: late May to early July. FLOWERS: yellow, flowerheads few to many in a branching terminal cluster, about ½" (1.3 cm) wide, rimmed with many narrowly rectangular, petal-like rays. PLANT: 1–3' (30–90 cm) tall; leaves basal, simple, obovate, margin entire, green with purple veining. HABITAT: woodlands.

Orange Hawkweed, Devil's Paintbrush
•*Hieracium aurantiacum* L.
•Aster family **Asteraceae**
FLOWERING SEASON: June–July. FLOWERS: orange to reddish orange; flowerheads few to several in a loose terminal cluster, up to 1" (2.5 cm) wide, rimmed with 2 to 3 layers of rectangular, minutely 5-toothed, petal-like rays. PLANT: 6–20" (15–50 cm) tall; leaves basal, simple, spathulate, pubescent, margin entire, green. HABITAT: fields, roadsides, and woodland openings. COMMENTS: although there are several yellow-flowerhead hawkweeds, this is the only species with orange flowers.

LEAVES ALTERNATE, SIMPLE

Elecampane
•*Inula helenium* L.
•Aster family **Asteraceae**
FLOWERING SEASON: mid-July to mid-August. FLOWERS: yellow; flowerheads several, terminal, 2–4" (5–10 cm) wide, rimmed with many very narrow, minutely 3-toothed, petal-like rays. PLANT: 2–6' (0.6–1.8 m) tall; leaves alternate and

Yellow Lotus / *Nelumbo lutea*

Orange Hawkweed, Devil's Paint-brush
/ *Hieracium aurantiacum*

Rattlesnake-weed / *Hieracium venosum*

Dandelion / *Taraxacum officinale*

Elecampane / *Inula helenium*

Coltsfoot / *Tussilago farfara*

basal, simple, broadly lance-shaped, rough textured, margin toothed, green. HABITAT: moist meadows.

Yellow Goat's-beard
•*Tragopogan pratensis* L.
•Aster family Asteraceae
FLOWERING SEASON: mid-May to late June. FLOWER: yellow, flowerhead solitary, terminal, 1½–2½" (3.8–6.3 cm) wide, rimmed with many oblong, minutely 5-toothed, petal-like rays. PLANT: 15–36" (37.5–90 cm) tall; leaves basal and alternate, simple, long and narrow, margin entire, green. HABITAT: fields and waste areas. COMMENTS: salsify, *Tragopogon porrifolius*, is a very similar plant with purplish flowerheads.

Black-eyed Susan
•*Rudbeckia hirta* L.
•Aster family Asteraceae
FLOWERING SEASON: July–August. FLOWERS: orangish yellow with a raised purplish brown center; flowerheads solitary to few, terminal, 2–4" (5–10 cm) wide, rimmed with 10 to 20 somewhat oblong, notch-tipped, petal-like rays. PLANT: 1–3' (30–90 cm) tall; leaves alternate, simple, lance-shaped, margin entire to slightly toothed, green. HABITAT: fields and meadows.

Sneezeweed
•*Helenium autumnale* L.
•Aster family Asteraceae
FLOWERING SEASON: late August through September. FLOWERS: yellow with a raised yellow globular center; flowerheads several to many, terminal, 1–2" (2.5–5 cm) wide, rimmed with 10 to 18 drooping, wedge-shaped, 3-lobed, petal-like rays. PLANT: 2–6' (0.6–1.8 m) tall; leaves alternate, simple, lance-shaped, margin toothed, green. HABITAT: swamps and wet meadows. COMMENTS: *Helenium flexosum*, also known as

sneezeweed, is a very similar plant with a raised brownish center.

LEAVES ALTERNATE, COMPOUND OR DEEPLY LOBED OR DIVIDED

Green-headed Coneflower
•*Rudbeckia laciniata* L.
•Aster family Asteraceae
FLOWERING SEASON: late July to early September. FLOWERS: yellow with a raised, ovoid, greenish-yellow center; flowerheads several, terminal, 2½–4" (6.3–10 cm) wide, rimmed with 6 to 10 drooping, somewhat oblong, petal-like rays. PLANT: 3–10' (0.9–3 m) tall; leaves alternate, simple, with 3 to 7 deeply cleft pinnate lobes, margin large-toothed, green. HABITAT: moist thickets.

LEAVES ALTERNATE OR OPPOSITE, OFTEN BOTH ON THE SAME PLANT

Thin-leaf Sunflower
•*Helianthus decapetalus* L.
•Aster family Asteraceae
FLOWERING SEASON: August–September. FLOWERS: yellow, flowerheads several, terminal, about 2½" (6.3 cm) wide, with 8 to 15 somewhat oblong, petal-like rays. PLANT: 1–5' (0.3–1.5 m) tall; leaves opposite or alternate, simple, broadly lance-shaped with a pointed tip, margin toothed, green. HABITAT: moist woodlands. COMMENTS: a very common woodland sunflower.

Giant Sunflower
•*Helianthus giganteus* L.
•Aster family Asteraceae
FLOWERING SEASON: September–October. FLOWERS: yellow; flowerheads several, terminal, about 2½" (6.3 cm) or more wide, rimmed with 10 to 20 or more lance-shaped, petal-like rays. PLANT: 3–12' (0.9–3.6 m) tall; leaves opposite and alternate on a rough stem,

Yellow Goat's-beard / *Tragopogan pratensis*

Black-eyed Susan / *Rudbeckia hirta*

Sneezeweed / *Helenium autumnale*

Green-headed Coneflower / *Rudbeckia laciniata*

Thin-leaf Sunflower / *Helianthus decapetalus*

Giant Sunflower / *Helianthus giganteus*

simple, lance-shaped, margin toothed, green. HABITAT: swamps and wet meadows.

Jerusalem Artichoke
•*Helianthus tuberosus* L.
•Aster family Asteraceae

FLOWERING SEASON: September through mid-October. FLOWERS: yellow; flowerheads several, terminal, about 3" (7.5 cm) wide, rimmed with 12 to 20 oblong, petal-like rays. PLANT: 6–12' (1.8–3.6 m) tall; leaves opposite and alternate on a rough stem, simple, ovate tapering to a pointed tip, margin toothed, green. HABITAT: creek and river banks and open moist soil. COMMENTS: prized for its edible, somewhat potato-like tuber.

LEAVES OPPOSITE, SIMPLE

Bur-marigold, Stick-tights
•*Bidens cernua* L.
•Aster family Asteraceae

FLOWERING SEASON: September. FLOWERS: yellow, flowerheads several to many, terminal and upper axial, ½–1" (1.3–2.5 cm) wide, rimmed with 6 to 10 short, petal-like rays. PLANT: 1–3' (30–90 cm) tall; leaves opposite, simple, narrowly lance-shaped, margin toothed, green. HABITAT: wet soil.

❦

FLOWERS NOT RADIALLY SYMMETRICAL; FLOWERS MINUTE, FILAMENTOUS, TUBULAR WITH NO PETAL-LIKE LOBES, OR WITH NO OBVIOUS PETAL-LIKE PARTS

LACKING TYPICAL LEAVES

Squawroot
•*Conopholis americana* (L.) Wallr.
•Broom-rape family Orobanchaceae

FLOWERING SEASON: June–July. FLOWERS: pale yellow, many completely covering a thick, cone-like stem, about ½"

(1.3 cm) long, tubular and 2-lipped; upper lip erect and hood-like; lower lip 3-lobed. PLANT: 3–10" (7.5–25 cm) tall; leaves absent, stem covered with large, straw-colored, lance-shaped scales. HABITAT: woodlands. COMMENTS: parasitic on tree roots.

Beechdrops
•*Epifagus virginiana* (L.) Bartr.
•Broom-rape family Orobanchaceae

FLOWERING SEASON: late August to early October. FLOWERS: yellowish with purplish brown stripes, many, alternate along branching stems, about ⁵⁄₁₆" (8 mm) long, tubular with 4 tiny triangular lobes. PLANT: 6–24" (15–60 cm) tall; leaves absent; stem yellowish brown. HABITAT: beech woodlands. COMMENTS: parasitic on beech tree roots.

AQUATIC

Horned Bladderwort
•*Utricularia cornuta* Michx.
•Bladderwort family Lentibulariaceae

FLOWERING SEASON: August. FLOWERS: yellow, 1 to 6, usually paired, terminal, about ¾" (1.9 cm) long, tubular and 2-lipped; upper lip small and erect; lower lip helmet-shaped with a conspicuous spur at the base. PLANT: aquatic, 3–10" (7.5–25 cm) tall; leaves submerged along an underwater stem, filamentous with small globular bladders. HABITAT: edges of ponds, fens, and other bodies of water. COMMENTS: the leaf bladders function to trap minute aquatic animals for food. Several other yellow bladderworts and one purple species also occur in New York State.

Beechdrops / *Epifagus virginiana*

Bur-marigold, Stick-tights / *Bidens cernua*

Squawroot / *Conopholis americana*

Jerusalem Artichoke / *Helianthus tuberosus*

Horned Bladderwort / *Utricularia cornuta*

LEAVES BASAL, SIMPLE

Golden-club
•*Orontium aquaticum* L.
•Arum family **Araceae**
FLOWERING SEASON: late April through May. FLOWERS: minute, many, clustered on a cylindrical 6–24" (15–60 cm) spike, the upper flowering portion bright yellow, the lower portion white. PLANT: 6–24" (15–60 cm) tall; leaves basal, simple, lance-shaped and long-stalked, margin entire, green. HABITAT: swamps, ponds, fens, often in standing water. COMMENTS: *Protected. Threatened. Do not disturb.* Primarily a coastal species but also found in two bog/fen locations in the Finger Lakes.

LEAVES ALTERNATE, SIMPLE

Yellow Violet
•*Viola pubescens* Ait.
•Violet family **Violaceae**
FLOWERING SEASON: May. FLOWERS: yellow with purple veining, few, terminal, up to ¾" (1.9 cm) wide, with 5 unequal rounded petals. PLANT: 5–20" (12.5–50 cm) tall; leaves basal and alternate, simple, broadly heart-shaped, margin toothed, green. HABITAT: woodlands.

Cypress Spurge
•*Euphorbia cyparissias* L.
•Spurge family **Euphorbiaceae**
FLOWERING SEASON: mid-May to mid-June. FLOWERS: yellowish green, becoming reddish orange in age, many, in about 2½" (6.3 cm) wide terminal or smaller axial flat-topped clusters; individual flowers minute, in small clusters above 2 showy, petal-like bracts. PLANT: up to 1' (30 cm) tall; leaves whorled (just below the flowers) or alternate, simple, long and narrow, margin entire, green. HABITAT: roadsides and waste areas. COMMENTS:

the milky sap of this and other spurges is poisonous.

Spotted Jewelweed, Touch-me-not
•*Impatiens capensis* Meerb.
•Touch-me-not family **Balsaminaceae**
FLOWERING SEASON: mid-July to early September. FLOWERS: orange-yellow mottled with reddish brown, solitary to several in leaf axils, ¾–1" (1.9–2.5 cm) long, tubular with a prominent curved basal spur and showy frontal lobes. PLANT: 2–5' (0.6–1.5 m) tall; leaves alternate, simple, ovate to elliptic, margin toothed, green. HABITAT: moist soil.

Pale Jewelweed, Touch-me-not
•*Impatiens pallida* Nutt.
•Touch-me-not family **Balsaminaceae**
FLOWERING SEASON: July–August. FLOWERS: pale yellow to yellow, sparingly mottled with reddish brown dots or dotless, solitary to several in leaf axils, 1–1¼" (2.5–3.1 cm) long, tubular with a prominent curved basal spur and showy frontal lobes. PLANT: 2–5' (0.6–1.5 m) tall; leaves alternate, simple, ovate to elliptic, margin toothed, green. HABITAT: moist soil.

Butter-and-eggs
•*Linaria vulgaris* Mill.
•Figwort family **Scrophulariaceae**
FLOWERING SEASON: mid-June through August. FLOWERS: pale yellow with orange on a portion of the lower lip, several in a narrow densely flowered terminal cluster, about 1–1¼" (2.5–3.1 cm) long, tubular with 2 lips and a long basal spur. PLANT: 1–2' (30–60 cm) tall; leaves alternate, simple, long and narrow, margin entire, green. HABITAT: fields, roadsides, and waste areas.

Golden-club / *Orontium aquaticum*

Yellow Violet / *Viola pubescens*

Butter-and-eggs / *Linaria vulgaris*

Cypress Spurge / *Euphorbia cyparissias*

Spotted Jewelweed, Touch-me-not / *Impatiens capensis*

Pale Jewelweed, Touch-me-not / *Impatiens pallida*

Wood-betony, Lousewort

- *Pedicularis canadensis* L.
- Figwort family **Scrophulariaceae**

FLOWERING SEASON: mid-May to early June. **FLOWERS:** bicolored; yellow and purplish brown, several in a dense terminal cluster, about ¾" (1.9 cm) long, tubular, 2-lipped; upper lip large and hood-shaped; lower lip 3-lobed. **PLANT:** 6–18" (15–45 cm) tall; leaves mostly alternate, simple, oblong and many-lobed, margin bluntly toothed, green. **HABITAT:** woodlands and along streams.

Blue-stem Goldenrod

- *Solidago caesia* L.
- Aster family **Asteraceae**

FLOWERING SEASON: September into October. **FLOWERS:** yellow, flowerheads many, in short axial clusters, up to ¼" (6 mm) high, rimmed with 5 tiny petal-like rays. **PLANT:** 1–3' (30–90 cm) tall; leaves alternate on a bluish to purple stem, simple, lance-shaped, margin sharply toothed, green. **HABITAT:** woodlands and thickets.

Late Goldenrod

- *Solidago gigantea* Ait.
- Aster family **Asteraceae**

FLOWERING SEASON: August–September. **FLOWERS:** yellow; flowerheads many in a showy branching terminal cluster, about ¼" (6 mm) high, rimmed with 7 to 15 tiny, petal-like rays. **PLANT:** 3–8' (0.9–2.4 m) tall; leaves alternate on a smooth stem, simple, lance-shaped, margin sharply toothed, green. **HABITAT:** open moist soil. **COMMENTS:** Canada goldenrod, *Solidago canadensis*, a very similar species of drier soils, has a pubescent stem and flowerheads about ⅛" (3 mm) high.

Yellow Lady's Slipper

- *Cypripedium parviflorum* Salisb.
- Orchid family **Orchidaceae**

FLOWERING SEASON: mid-May to mid-June. **FLOWERS:** lip yellow, sepals and petals from yellowish green (*var. pubescens*) to dark reddish brown (*var. parviflorum* and *makasin*), 1 to 2, terminal; lip about ¾–1¼" (1.9–3.1 cm) long in *var. parviflorum* and *var. makasin*, up to about 2" (5 cm) long in *var. pubescens*, pouch-like. **PLANT:** 1–2' (30–60 cm) tall; leaves 3 to 5, alternate, simple, lance-shaped to nearly round, margin entire, green. **HABITAT:** variable, from dry to more often moist woodlands, swamps, and wooded fens.

Crested Fringed Orchid

- *Platanthera cristata* (Michx.) Lindl.
- Orchid family **Orchidaceae**

FLOWERING SEASON: late July to early August. **FLOWERS:** orange, 40 to 80 in a dense terminal cluster, about ⅜" (9 mm) tall and wide, with 5 small petal-like parts and a larger single-lobed, conspicuously fringed lip with a slender basal spur. **PLANT:** 8–24" (20–60 cm) tall; leaves alternate, simple, lance-shaped, margin entire, green. **HABITAT:** sandy soil in meadows or open pine woods, sometimes quite close to the ocean. **COMMENTS:** *protected. Endangered. Do not disturb.* Found in southeastern New York. Very similar creamy white orchids found in eastern Long Island have been proposed as a separate species, tentatively labeled *Platanthera pallida*.

Yellow Lady's Slipper / *Cypripedium parviflorum*

Blue-stem Goldenrod / *Solidago caesia*

Crested Fringed Orchid / *Platanthera cristata*

Wood-betony, Lousewort / *Pedicularis canadensis*

Late Goldenrod / *Solidago gigantea*

Platanthera pallida

LEAVES ALTERNATE, COMPOUND OR DEEPLY DIVIDED

Early Meadow-rue
- *Thalictrum dioicum* L.
- Crowfoot family **Ranunculaceae**

FLOWERING SEASON: late April to mid-May. FLOWERS: greenish to yellowish, several to many in a terminal cluster, about ¼" (6 mm) long, composed of a tassel-like mass of yellowish thread-like stamens and about 5 tiny petal-like sepals. PLANT: 1–2' (30–60 cm) tall; leaves alternate, compound with numerous leaflets; leaflets rounded with 5 to 9 lobes, green. HABITAT: woodlands.

Black Medick
- *Medicago lupulina* L.
- Bean family **Fabaceae**

FLOWERING SEASON: June–August. FLOWERS: yellow, many, in oblong ¼" (6 mm) tall flowerheads; individual flowers tiny. PLANT: often prostrate, up to 2' (60 cm) long; leaves alternate, compound with 3 leaflets; leaflets obovate, margins minutely toothed, green; fruit a cluster of black, tightly spiraled pods. HABITAT: fields, lawns, and waste areas. COMMENTS: often found in stunted form in lawns.

Bird's-foot Trefoil
- *Lotus corniculata* L.
- Bean family **Fabaceae**

FLOWERING SEASON: late May into September. FLOWERS: yellow, many, 3 to 12 in rounded clusters scattered throughout the plant, about ⅝" (1.6 cm) long, pea-like. PLANT: trailing or ascending, 3–24" (7.5–60 cm) long; leaves alternate, compound with 3 leaflets; leaflets obovate, margins entire, green. HABITAT: meadows, roadsides, and waste areas. COMMENTS: seeds in several slender pods that resemble a bird's foot.

Yellow Sweet-clover
- *Melilotus altissima* Thuill.
- Bean family **Fabaceae**

FLOWERING SEASON: June–August. FLOWERS: yellow, many, in slender 2–4" (5–10 cm) long, often 1-sided axial clusters, about ¼" (6 mm) long, narrowly pea-like. PLANT: 3–5' (0.9–1.5 m) tall; leaves alternate, compound with 3 leaflets; leaflets narrowly oblong, margin toothed, green. HABITAT: fields, roadsides, and waste areas.

Pineapple-weed
- *Matricaria discoidea* DC.
- Aster family **Asteraceae**

FLOWERING SEASON: late May into August. FLOWERS: greenish yellow; flowerheads many, terminal and axial, up to 5/16" (8 mm) wide, appearing like a small daisy without petals. PLANT: 6–18" (15–45 cm) tall; leaves alternate, simple, pinnately divided into many narrow lobes, margin toothed, green, giving off a pineapple-like fragrance when torn. HABITAT: waste areas, meadows, and roadsides.

LEAVES OPPOSITE, SIMPLE

Horse-balm
- *Collinsonia canadensis* L.
- Mint family **Lamiaceae**

FLOWERING SEASON: August. FLOWERS: light yellow, several to many in a loose terminal cluster, about ½" (1.3 cm) long, tubular with 2 lips; upper lip 3-lobed; lower lip 2-lobed; lemony fragrance. PLANT: 2–5' (0.6–1.5 m) tall; leaves opposite on a square stem, simple, ovate, margin coarsely and sharply toothed, green. HABITAT: moist woodlands.

Early Meadow-rue / *Thalictrum dioicum*

Horse-balm / *Collinsonia canadensis*

Bird's-foot Trefoil / *Lotus corniculata*

Black Medick / *Medicago lupulina*

Yellow Sweet-clover / *Melilotus altissima*

Pineapple-weed / *Matricaria discoidea*

Dotted Horsemint
•*Monarda punctata* L.
•Mint family **Lamiaceae**
FLOWERING SEASON: late July to early September. **FLOWERS:** yellowish with purple spots, many, in circular axillary or terminal clusters, about 1" (2.5 cm) long, tubular with 2 elongated lips; upper lip 2-lobed, lower lip 3-lobed. **PLANT:** 2–3' (60–90 cm) tall; leaves opposite on a square stem, simple, lance-shaped, margin toothed, green. **HABITAT:** sandy soils, frequently found along the ocean.

Bush Honeysuckle
•*Diervilla lonicera* Mill.
•Honeysuckle family **Caprifoliaceae**
FLOWERING SEASON: June. **FLOWERS:** yellow, 1 to 5 in terminal clusters, about ¾" (1.9 cm) long, tubular with 5 recurved petal-like lobes. **PLANT:** shrub, 2–4' (0.6–1.2 m) tall; leaves opposite, simple, lance-shaped, margin minutely toothed, green. **HABITAT:** woodlands.

Early Fly Honeysuckle
•*Lonicera canadensis* Bartr.
•Honeysuckle family **Caprifoliaceae**
FLOWERING SEASON: May. **FLOWERS:** yellow to greenish yellow, in axial pairs, about ¾" (1.9 cm) long, funnel-shaped with 5 equal lobes. **PLANT:** shrub, 2–5' (0.6–1.5 m) tall; leaves opposite, simple, oval, margin entire, green. **HABITAT:** woodlands.

Tartarian Honeysuckle
•*Lonicera tartarica* L.
•Honeysuckle family **Caprifoliaceae**
FLOWERING SEASON: mid-May to mid-June. **FLOWERS:** pink to white or yellowish, many, in axial pairs, about ¾" (1.9 cm) long, tubular with 5 unequal, narrow, petal-like lobes. **PLANT:** shrub, 5–10' (1.5–3 m) tall; leaves opposite, simple, ovate, margin entire, green. **HABITAT:** hedgerows, thickets, and open woodlots.

Japanese Honeysuckle
•*Lonicera japonica* Thunb.
•Honeysuckle family **Caprifoliaceae**
FLOWERING SEASON: July–August. **FLOWERS:** white to yellow, in pairs in upper axils, about 1" (2.5 cm) long, tubular and 2-lipped, upper lip narrow, 1-lobed, recurved; lower lip broad, 4-lobed, recurved. **PLANT:** vine-like; leaves opposite, simple, ovate, margin entire, green. **HABITAT:** woodlands, swamps, and thickets. **COMMENTS:** escaped from cultivation and sometimes a serious pest.

Dotted Horsemint / *Monarda punctata*

Bush Honeysuckle / *Dierville lonicera*

Tartarian Honeysuckle / *Lonicera tartarica*

Early Fly Honeysuckle / *Lonicera canadensis*

Japanese Honeysuckle / *Lonicera japonica*

PART FOUR

GREEN FLOWERS

❧

FLOWERS SYMMETRICAL, WITH 4 PETALS OR PETAL-LIKE PARTS

TYPICAL LEAVES LACKING, PARASITIC ON BLACK SPRUCE

Dwarf Mistletoe
• *Arceuthobium pusillum* C. Peck
• Mistletoe family **Viscaceae**
FLOWERING SEASON: late April through early June. FLOWERS: greenish, many, solitary or paired in axils; dioecious (male and female flowers different, in this species typically found on separate host trees); male flowers about ⅛" (3 mm) wide; female flowers tiny, much smaller than the scale-like leaves; male flowers as large or larger than the scale-like leaves, with 4 pointed, petal-like divisions. PLANT: parasitic, usually on twigs of black spruce, stem ⅛–¾" (3–19 mm) long; leaves simple, scale-like, nearly round, tiny, tightly appressed to the stem, greenish brown. HABITAT: fens and bogs. COMMENTS: a black spruce, *Picea mariana*, infected with dwarf mistletoe, has much denser foliage than an uninfected tree.

～

FLOWERS SYMMETRICAL, WITH 5 PETALS OR PETAL-LIKE PARTS

LEAVES ALTERNATE, COMPOUND

Poison Ivy
• *Toxicodendron radicans* (L.) Kuntze
• Sumac family **Anacardiaceae**
FLOWERING SEASON: June. FLOWERS: green, many in 1–3" (2.5–7.5 cm) long, loose axial clusters, about ⅛" (3 mm) wide, with 5 tiny rounded petals. PLANT: woody vine, up to 20' (6 m) or more long; leaves alternate, compound with 3 leaflets; leaflets ovate, margins entire or with a few large teeth, green. HABITAT: swamps, woodlands, and roadsides.

COMMENTS: contact with any part of this plant may cause severe dermatitis.

LEAVES OPPOSITE OR WHORLED, COMPOUND

Ginseng
• *Panax quinquefolius* L.
• Ginseng family **Araliaceae**
FLOWERING SEASON: late June to mid-July. FLOWERS: greenish yellow, 6 to 20 in a small, rounded terminal cluster, about ¹⁄₁₆" (1.6 mm) wide, with 5 inconspicuous petals and 5 prominent stamens. PLANT: 8–15" (20–37.5 cm) tall; leaves 3, whorled about the stem, palmately compound with 5 leaflets; leaflets ovate with a pointed tip, margins irregularly toothed, green. HABITAT: woodlands. COMMENTS: *Commercially exploited. Do not disturb.*

～

FLOWERS SYMMETRICAL, WITH 6 PETALS OR PETAL-LIKE PARTS

LEAVES ALTERNATE, SIMPLE

Carrion-flower
• *Smilax herbacea* L.
• Greenbrier family **Smilacaceae**
FLOWERING SEASON: June. FLOWERS: green, many, in rounded, long-stemmed axial clusters, about ⅜" (9 mm) wide, with 6 narrowly lance-shaped, petal-like divisions and several conspicuous, filamentous, white-tipped stamens; unpleasantly fragrant. PLANT: climbing vine, 3–6' (0.9–1.8 m) long; leaves alternate on a smooth herbaceous stem, simple, ovate, often with a slightly heart-shaped base, margin entire, green. HABITAT: woodlands, thickets, and along waterways. COMMENTS: the common name refers to the flowers' odor of rotten meat. Other *Smilax* species have armed woody stems: the stem of the bristly greenbrier, *S. hispi-*

Poison Ivy / *Toxicodendron radicans*

Black Spruce (right) infected by Dwarf Mistletoe,
Arceuthobium pusillum; uninfected tree on left

Ginseng / *Panax quinquefolius*

Carrion-flower / *Smilax herbacea*

da, is covered with numerous tiny prickles; the stem of horse-brier, *S. rotundifolia*, has fewer thorns, which are stout, flattened, and rose-like.

Yellow Mandarin

• *Disporum lanuginosum* (Michx.) Nichols.
• Lily family **Liliaceae**

FLOWERING SEASON: late May to early June. FLOWERS: yellowish green, several, usually found in pairs on stem tips, about ⅝" (1.6 cm) long, perianth with 6 long, narrow parts. PLANT: 1½–2½' (45–75 cm) tall; leaves alternate along an angularly twisted stalk, simple, broadly lance-shaped with a rounded base, margin entire, green. HABITAT: woodlands.

False Hellebore

• *Veratrum viride* Ait.
• Lily family **Liliaceae**

FLOWERING SEASON: mid-June to mid-July. FLOWERS: yellowish green, many in an 8–24" (20–60 cm) branching terminal cluster, up to 1" (2.5 cm) wide, perianth with 6 oblong, petal-like parts. PLANT: 2–8' (0.6–2.4 m) tall; leaves alternate, simple, broadly oval, margin entire, green. HABITAT: swamps and wet woods.

❧

FLOWERS NOT RADIALLY SYM-METRICAL; FLOWERS MINUTE, FILAMENTOUS, TUBULAR WITH NO PETAL-LIKE LOBES OR WITH NO OBVIOUS PETAL-LIKE PARTS

LEAVES BASAL, SIMPLE

Loesel's Twayblade

• *Liparis loeselii* (L.) L. Rich.
• Orchid family **Orchidaceae**

FLOWERING SEASON: late June through mid-July. FLOWERS: yellowish green, 2 to 12 in a loose, slender terminal cluster, about ⅜" (10 mm) tall, with 5 very narrow petals and sepals and an oblong lip. PLANT: 2–8" (5–20 cm) tall; leaves 2, basal, simple, oblong, margin entire, green. HABITAT: moist soils (from fens to roadside ditches). COMMENTS: the lily-leaved twayblade, *Liparis lilifolia*, has flowers about twice as large with a mauve to purplish lip.

Sweetflag, Calamus

• *Acorus americanus* (Raf.) Raf.
• Arum family **Araceae**

FLOWERING SEASON: late May through June. FLOWERS: greenish yellow, minute, many clustered on a 2–3½" (5–8.8 cm) long, finger-like projection found on the lower third of a leaf-like flower stem. PLANT: 2–6' (0.6–1.8 m) tall; leaves basal, simple, long and narrow, margin entire, pale green. HABITAT: swamps, moist meadows, and along streams.

Arrowleaf, Tuckahoe, Arrow Arum

• *Peltandra virginica* (L.) Schott ex Schott & Endl.
• Arum family **Araceae**

FLOWERING SEASON: mid-June to mid-July. FLOWERS: minute, many on an erect cylindrical spike almost entirely enclosed in a green 4–8" (10–20 cm) tall sheath that appears like a rolled up leaf. PLANT: 6–30" (15–75 cm) tall; leaves basal, simple, arrowhead-shaped and long-stemmed, margin entire, green. HABITAT: swamps, drainage ditches, edges of ponds and lakes, often in standing water.

Loesel's Twayblade / *Liparis loeselii*

False Hellebore / *Veratrum viride*

Sweetflag, Calamus / *Acorus americanus*

Yellow Mandarin / *Disporum lanuginosum*

Arrowleaf, Tuckahoe, Arrow Arum / *Peltandra virginica*

LEAVES BASAL, COMPOUND OR DEEPLY DIVIDED

Jack-in-the-pulpit

- *Arisaema triphyllum* (L.) Schott ex Schott & Endl.
- Arum family **Araceae**

FLOWERING SEASON: May through early June. **FLOWERS:** minute, many clustered on an erect, finger-like projection enclosed by a leaf-like sheath; sheath appearing tubular at the base, the upper portion arching forward over the flowering spike; green, usually with purple stripes. **PLANT:** 10–36" (25–90 cm) tall; leaves 1 or 2, basal, long-stalked, each with 3 leaflets; leaflets broadly lance-shaped, margins entire, green. **HABITAT:** woodlands.

Green Dragon, Dragon-root

- *Arisaema dracontium* (L.) Schott ex Schott & Endl.
- Arum family **Araceae**

FLOWERING SEASON: June. **FLOWERS:** minute, many on an erect 1–2" (2.5–5 cm) long, cylindrical yellowish spike tapering upward another 7" (17.5 cm) above the flowering portion, the lower portion enclosed in a leaf-like sheath. **PLANT:** 8–32" (20–80 cm) tall; leaf usually solitary, basal, long-stalked, with 5 to 17 leaflets in the upper portion, which is usually oriented parallel to the ground; leaflets mostly arranged on the same side of the stalk, oblong, margins entire, green. **HABITAT:** moist woodlands and along streams.

LEAVES ALTERNATE, SIMPLE

Frost Grape

- *Vitis riparia* Michx.
- Grape family **Vitaceae**

FLOWERING SEASON: June. **FLOWERS:** pale green, many in loose axial clusters about 3" (7.5 cm) long; individual flow-ers minute. **PLANT:** woody vine, up to 25' (7.5 m) or more long; leaves alternate, simple, broadly ovate with 3 to 7 lobes, margin coarsely toothed, green, smooth on both surfaces. **HABITAT:** hedgerows, woodlands, and riverbanks. **COMMENTS:** fox grape, *Vitis lambrusca*, which has many cultivated varieties, has broader leaves with a densely pubescent lower surface.

Small Solomon's-Seal

- *Polygonatum biflorum* (Walt.) Ell.
- Lily family **Liliaceae**

FLOWERING SEASON: late May to early June. **FLOWERS:** yellowish green, several, found singly or in pairs (occasionally in groups of 3 or 4) in axils, about ½" (1.3 cm) long, tubularly bell-shaped with 6 small pointed teeth, pendant. **PLANT:** 8–36" (20–90 cm) long, leaves alternate, simple, broadly lance-shaped, margin entire, green. **HABITAT:** woodlands. **COMMENTS:** hairy Solomon's-Seal, *Polygonatum pubescens*, has hairy veins on the underside of the leaves. *P. biflorum* has smooth veins.

Helleborine Orchid

- *Epipactis helleborine* (L.) Crantz
- Orchid family **Orchidaceae**

FLOWERING SEASON: mid-July through late August. **FLOWERS:** pale to olive-green with reddish brown tints, 15 to 35 or more in a slender terminal cluster, about ⅗" (15 cm) tall and wide, with 5 broadly lance-shaped, petal-like parts and a cup-shaped lip. **PLANT:** 10–24" (25–60 cm) or more tall; leaves alternate, simple, broadly lance-shaped, margin entire, green. **HABITAT:** woodlands. **COMMENTS:** the only alien orchid found in New York. First recorded near Syracuse in 1879 and now the most commonly encountered woodland orchid in the state.

15 CM

Green Dragon, Dragon-root / *Arisaema dracontium*

Small Solomon's-Seal / *Polygonatum biflorum*

Helleborine Orchid / *Epipactis helleborine*

Frost Grape / *Vitis riparia*

Jack-in-the-pulpit / *Arisaema triphyllum*

Bayard's Malaxis
•*Malaxis bayardii* Fern.
•Orchid family **Orchidaceae**
FLOWERING SEASON: July–August. **FLOW-ERS:** green to yellowish green, with up to 50 flowers in a tall cylindrical terminal cluster, about ¼" (6 mm) tall; prominent, deeply notched lip with somewhat horn-like lobes at the base. **PLANT:** 4–10" (10–25 cm) tall; leaf solitary on the stem, simple, broadly obovate, margin entire, green. **HABITAT:** sandy or rocky soil in dry woodlands. **COMMENTS:** *protected. Endangered. Do not disturb.* Green adder's-mouth, *Malaxis unifolia*, which has a funnel-shaped flower cluster, and a lip that is heart-shaped at the base, is found in moister soils. The flowers of white adder's-mouth, *M. brachypoda*, so short-stalked that they hug the stem, have a single tipped lip.

LEAVES ALTERNATE, COMPOUND OR DEEPLY DIVIDED

Common Mugwort, Wormwood
•*Artemisia vulgaris* L.
•Aster family **Asteraceae**
FLOWERING SEASON: late August through September. **FLOWERS:** greenish, flower-heads many in the upper leaf axils, about ³⁄₁₆" (5 mm) wide, oblong. **PLANT:** 1–3½' (0.3–1.1 m) tall; leaves alternate, pinnate-ly compound into sharply toothed lobes, margins coarsely toothed, dark green above, white and densely tomentose beneath. **HABITAT:** waste areas.

LEAVES ALTERNATE AND OPPOSITE ON THE SAME PLANT, COMPOUND OR DEEPLY DIVIDED

Ragweed
•*Ambrosia artemisiifolia* L.
•Aster family **Asteraceae**
FLOWERING SEASON: mid-August to mid-September. **FLOWERS:** yellow-green, flowerheads many, in 1–6" (2.5–15 cm) long, slender terminal and upper axial clusters about ³⁄₁₆" (5 mm) wide. **PLANT:** 1–6' (0.3–1.8 m) tall; upper leaves alter-nate, lower leaves mostly opposite, sim-ple, oblong to lance-shaped, margin deeply pinnately cleft and coarsely toothed, green. **HABITAT:** fields, road-sides, and waste areas.

LEAVES OPPOSITE OR WHORLED, SIMPLE

Stinging Nettle
•*Urtica dioica* L.
•Nettle family **Urticaceae**
FLOWERING SEASON: August–September. **FLOWERS:** pale green, many in long, very slender axial clusters, (about as long as nearby leaves), minute. **PLANT:** 2–7' (0.6–2.1 m) tall; leaves opposite, simple, narrowly ovate to lance-shaped with a rounded to slightly heart-shaped base, sharply toothed, green. **HABITAT:** fields, farmyards, waste areas, and swamps. **COMMENTS:** beware of touching. Nettles are covered with numerous tiny but mad-deningly stinging hairs. Wood-nettle, *Laportea canadensis*, is the only stinging nettle with alternate leaves. It has broad, ovate leaves and broad, spreading flower clusters; it is found in rich, moist wood-lands.

Large Whorled Pogonia
•*Isotria verticillata* (Muhl. ex Willd.) Raf.
•Orchid family **Orchidaceae**
FLOWERING SEASON: late May through early June. **FLOWER:** greenish yellow, solitary, terminal, about 2¾" (6.9 cm) tall, center of flower appearing tubular, about ¾" (1.9 cm) long, framed by 3 very long and narrow brownish sepals. **PLANT:** 5–12" (12.5–30 cm) tall; leaves 5 or 6 in a single whorl, simple, broadly lance-shaped, margin entire, green. **HABITAT:** damp to dry woodlands and

Common Mugwort, Wormwood / *Artemisia vulgaris*

Large Whorled Pogonia / *Isotria verticillata*

Bayard's Malaxis / *Malaxis bayardii*

Ragweed / *Ambrosia artemisiifolia*

Stinging Nettle / *Urtica dioica*

swampy edges of fens. COMMENTS: the small whorled pogonia, *Isotria medeoloides*, has all greenish yellow floral parts and much shorter sepals.

LEAVES OPPOSITE OR WHORLED, COMPOUND

Wild Sarsaparilla
•*Aralia nudicaulis* L.
•Ginseng family **Araliaceae**
FLOWERING SEASON: mid-May to mid-June. FLOWERS: greenish, many, on each of usually 3 circular clusters arising from a single stalk, about ⅛" (3 mm) wide, inconspicuous. PLANT : 12–15" (30–45 cm) tall; leaf solitary, basal, divided so as to appear as 3 whorled, pinnately compound leaves; leaflets usually 5 per section, of unequal size, ovate with a pointed tip, margins toothed, green. HABITAT: woodlands.

Wild Sarsaparilla / *Aralia nudicaulis*

PART FIVE

BLUE TO VIOLET FLOWERS
INCLUDING BLUISH PURPLE

❧

FLOWERS SYMMETRICAL, WITH 3 PETALS OR PETAL-LIKE PARTS

LEAVES BASAL, SIMPLE

Wild Iris, Blue Flag, Fleur-de-lis
•*Iris versicolor* L.
•Iris family **Iridaceae**
FLOWERING SEASON: June through early July. **FLOWERS:** violet-blue, several terminal on an upright stem, about 3" (7.5 cm) wide, perianth 6-parted, 3 outer parts broadly paddle-shaped with downturned tips and yellow and white veining, 3 inner parts smaller, narrower, somewhat erect. **PLANT:** 2–3' (60–90 cm) tall; leaves basal, simple, long and narrow, margin entire, bluish green. **HABITAT:** marshes, wet meadows, and along bodies of water.

FLOWERS SYMMETRICAL, WITH 4 PETALS OR PETAL-LIKE PARTS

LEAVES OPPOSITE OR WHORLED, SIMPLE

Fringed Gentian
•*Gentianopsis crinita* (Froel.) Ma
•Gentian family **Gentianaceae**
FLOWERING SEASON: September–October **FLOWERS:** blue, several, terminal, about 2" (5 cm) long, tubular with 4 rounded, heavily fringed apical petal-like lobes. **PLANT:** about 1–3' (30–90 cm) tall; leaves opposite, simple, lance-shaped with a rounded base, margin entire, green. **HABITAT:** moist meadows and roadsides.

Bluets
•*Houstonia caerulea* L.
•Madder family **Rubiaceae**
FLOWERING SEASON: early May to mid-June. **FLOWERS:** pale violet to white with a yellow center, few to several, terminal, about 7⁄16" (1.1 cm) wide, tubular with 4

sharply pointed, petal-like lobes. **PLANT:** 3–7" (7.5–17.5 cm) tall; leaves basal and opposite, simple, narrowly paddle-shaped, margin entire, green. **HABITAT:** open grassy areas, often at higher elevations.

FLOWERS SYMMETRICAL, WITH 5 PETALS OR PETAL-LIKE PARTS

LEAVES BASAL, SIMPLE

Marsh-rosemary, Sea-lavender
•*Limonium carolinianum* (Walt.) Britt.
•Leadwort family **Plumbaginaceae**
FLOWERING SEASON: August–September. **FLOWERS:** lavender, pale purple, many in a large, loose terminal cluster, tiny, with 5 rounded petals. **PLANT:** 1–2' (30–60 cm) tall; leaves basal, simple, broadly lance-shaped with a long stalk, margin entire or minutely wavy, green. **HABITAT:** coastal meadows.

LEAVES ALTERNATE, SIMPLE

Forget-me-not
•*Myosotis scorpioides* L.
•Borage family **Boraginaceae**
FLOWERING SEASON: May–July. **FLOWERS:** pale blue with a yellow center, many, in long, slender clusters, about ¼" (6 mm) wide, with 5 nearly round, petal-like lobes. **PLANT:** 6–18" (15–45 cm) tall; leaves alternate, simple, oblong, minutely hairy, margin entire, green. **HABITAT:** along brooks, marshes, and drainage ditches. **COMMENTS:** several very similar species, some with white flowers, are also found in New York.

Bluets / *Houstonia caerulea*

Wild Iris, Blue Flag, Fleur-de-lis / *Iris versi-color*

Marsh-rosemary, Sea-lavender / *Limonium car-olinianum*

Fringed Gentian / *Gentianopsis crinita*

Forget-me-not / *Myosotis scorpioides*

LEAVES ALTERNATE, DEEPLY LOBED

Nightshade

- *Solanum dulcamara* L.
- Nightshade family **Solanaceae**

FLOWERING SEASON: early June into August. **FLOWERS:** purple, blue, or white with a protruding yellow center, several, in loose clusters, about ½" (1.3 cm) wide, corolla with 5 deeply recurved, sharply pointed, petal-like lobes, often nodding. **PLANT:** vine-like, 2–8' (0.6–2.4 m) long; leaves alternate, simple, 3-lobed, central lobe large, broadly tear-shaped, lateral lobes small and lance-shaped, margin entire, green; fruit green to bright red when ripe, tomato-like, *poisonous*. **HABITAT:** roadsides, waste areas, and thickets. **COMMENTS:** often found with flowers and fruit simultaneously.

LEAVES OPPOSITE, SIMPLE

Common Periwinkle

- *Vinca minor* L.
- Dogbane family **Apocynaceae**

FLOWERING SEASON: late April through May. **FLOWERS:** blue or occasionally white or pinkish, few, solitary in axils, about 1" (2.5 cm) wide, with 5 wide, blunt, petal-like parts. **PLANT:** prostrate, stems 6–24" (15–60 cm) long; leaves opposite, simple, oblong, margin entire, green. **HABITAT:** escaped from cultivation into woodlands and meadows.

Blue Phlox

- *Phlox divaricata* L.
- Phlox family **Polemoniaceae**

FLOWERING SEASON: mid-May to mid-June. **FLOWERS:** blue, several to many in a rounded terminal cluster, about 1" (2.5 cm) wide, tubular, with 5 paddle-shaped, petal-like lobes. **PLANT:** 12–20" (30–50 cm) tall; leaves opposite, simple, lance-shaped, margin entire, green.

HABITAT: woodlands.

Blue Vervain

- *Verbena hastata* L.
- Verbena family **Verbenaceae**

FLOWERING SEASON: July through early September. **FLOWERS:** blue, many, in slender terminal clusters, about ⅛" (3 mm) wide, tubular with 5 tiny lobes. **PLANT:** 3–7' (0.9–2.1 m) tall; leaves opposite, simple, lance-shaped, margin toothed, green. **HABITAT:** moist fields, meadows, and drainage ditches.

FLOWERS SYMMETRICAL, WITH 6 PETALS OR PETAL-LIKE PARTS

LEAVES BASAL, SIMPLE

Blue-eyed Grass

- *Sisyrinchium angustifolium* Mill.
- Iris family **Iridaceae**

FLOWERING SEASON: late May through June. **FLOWERS:** violet-blue with a yellow center, 1 to 3, terminal on an upright 2-edged stem, about ¾" (1.9 cm) wide, perianth with 6 oblong, bristle-tipped, petal-like parts. **PLANT:** 3–14" (7.5–35 cm) tall; leaves basal, simple, long and narrow, margin entire, green, flowering stem with a long, leaf-like bract halfway up the stem. **HABITAT:** moist fields and meadows.

LEAVES ALTERNATE, SIMPLE

Creeping Bellflower

- *Campanula rapunculoides* L.
- Bluebell family **Campanulaceae**

FLOWERING SEASON: late June to early August. **FLOWERS:** blue to violet, many in a slender 1-sided terminal cluster, about 1 ¼" (3.1 cm) long, bell-shaped with 5 somewhat flaring triangular lobes. **PLANT:** about 1–3' (30–90 cm) tall; leaves alternate, simple, broadly lance-shaped, margin toothed, green. **HABITAT:** fields, roadsides, and waste areas.

Blue-eyed Grass / *Sisyrinchium angustifolium*

Creeping Bellflower / *Campanula rapunculoides*

Nightshade / *Solanum dulcamara*

Blue Vervain / *Verbena hastata*

Blue Phlox / *Phlox divaricata*

Common Periwinkle / *Vinca minor*

Harebell, Bluebell

• *Campanula rotundifolia* L.
• Bluebell family **Campanulaceae**
FLOWERING SEASON: late June through August. **FLOWERS:** blue, few to several, in slender 1-sided upper axial clusters, up to 1" (2.5 cm) long, bell-shaped with 5 triangular lobes. **PLANT:** 6–39" (15–97.5 cm) or more tall; leaves basal and alternate, simple, basal leaves broadly heart-shaped; stem leaves very narrow, green. **HABITAT:** moist rocky areas.

~

FLOWERS SYMMETRICAL, WITH 7 OR MORE PETALS OR PETAL-LIKE PARTS

LEAVES ALTERNATE, SIMPLE

Chicory

• *Cichorium intybus* L.
• Aster family **Asteraceae**
FLOWERING SEASON: mid-June to mid-September. **FLOWERS:** blue or occasionally white; flowerheads many, in clusters of 1 to 4 along the branching stems, about 1¼" (3.1 cm) wide, rimmed with many oblong, minutely 5-toothed, petal-like rays. **PLANT:** 1–3' (30–90 cm) tall; leaves basal and alternate, simple, lance-shaped, margin unevenly toothed, green. **HABITAT:** fields, roadsides, and waste areas.

Blue Lettuce

• *Lactuca biennis* (Moench) Fern.
• Aster family **Asteraceae**
FLOWERING SEASON: August through early September. **FLOWERS:** blue; flowerheads many in a large, branching, dense terminal cluster, about ⅛" (3 mm) wide, rimmed with many minutely 5-toothed, petal-like rays. **PLANT:** 3–12' (0.9–3.6 m) tall; leaves alternate, simple, with several large, triangular, pinnately arranged lobes, margin coarsely and unevenly

toothed, green. **HABITAT:** moist meadows and woodland clearings.

Blue Wood Aster

• *Aster cordifolius* L.
• Aster family **Asteraceae**
FLOWERING SEASON: September–October. **FLOWERS:** white, violet, or blue, with a pinkish to purplish center, flowerheads many, terminal and upper axial, ½–¾" (1.3–1.9 cm) wide, rimmed with 10 to 20 petal-like rays. **PLANT:** 1–5' (0.3–1.5 m) tall; leaves alternate and basal; upper leaves lance-shaped; lower and basal leaves heart-shaped with a deeply cleft base, margin toothed, green. **HABITAT:** woods and thickets.

~

FLOWERS NOT RADIALLY SYMMETRICAL; FLOWERS MINUTE, FILAMENTOUS, TUBULAR WITH NO PETAL-LIKE LOBES, OR WITH NO OBVIOUS PETAL-LIKE PARTS

LEAVES BASAL, SIMPLE

Pickerel-weed

• *Pontederia cordata* L.
• Pickerel-weed family **Pontederiaceae**
FLOWERING SEASON: late July–August. **FLOWERS:** blue, many on a densely flowered 1–3" (2.5–7.5 cm) long, cylindrical terminal cluster, about ½" (1.3 cm) wide, perianth tubular and 2-lipped, each lip with 3 long, petal-like lobes, the central lip of the upper lobe with 2 large yellow spots. **PLANT:** 1–4' (0.3–1.2 m) tall; leaves mostly basal, simple, narrowly heart-shaped, margin entire, green. **HABITAT:** aquatic, in the shallow borders of ponds and streams.

Blue Wood Aster / *Aster cordifolius*

Chicory / *Cichorium intybus*

Harebell, Bluebell / *Campanula rotundifolia*

Pickerel-weed / *Pontederia cordata*

Blue Lettuce / *Lactuca biennis*

Butterwort
- *Pinguicula vulgaris* L.
- Bladderwort family **Lentibulariaceae**

FLOWERING SEASON: June. FLOWER: violet-purple, solitary, terminal, about ½" (1.3 cm) long, tubular with a basal spur and 2-lipped; upper lip 2-lobed, lower lip 3-lobed. PLANT: 2–6" (5–15 cm) tall; leaves basal, simple, ovate, margin entire, yellowish green, upper surface greasy. HABITAT: wet rocky areas. COMMENTS: *protected. Threatened. Do not disturb.*

Great Spurred Violet, Selkirk Violet
- *Viola selkirkii* Pursh ex Goldie
- Violet family **Violaceae**

FLOWERING SEASON: May. FLOWERS: violet, several, on individual stalks, about ½" (1.3 cm) wide, with 5 unequal rounded petals and a thick, blunt spur at the base. PLANT: 1½–4" (3.8–10 cm) tall; leaves basal, simple, broadly ovate to nearly round with a deeply cleft, heart-shaped base, margin finely toothed, green. HABITAT: moist woodlands.

LEAVES ALTERNATE, SIMPLE

Long-spurred Violet
Viola rostrata Pursh
Violet family **Violaceae**

FLOWERING SEASON: May. FLOWERS: pale violet with blue veining, several, terminal, about ¾" (1.9 cm) wide, with 5 unequal rounded petals and a long, slender spur at the base. PLANT: 2–7" (5–17.5 cm) tall; leaves basal and alternate, simple, somewhat heart-shaped, margin toothed, green. HABITAT: woodlands.

Viper's Bugloss
- *Echium vulgare* L.
- Borage family **Boraginaceae**

FLOWERING SEASON: mid-June to mid-August. FLOWERS: bright blue to purplish, several to many in tall, slender clusters, up to 1" (2.5 cm) long, tubular with 5 unequal rounded lobes. PLANT: 12–30" (30–75 cm) tall; leaves alternate, simple, narrowly oblong, hairy, margin entire, green. HABITAT: fields and waste areas.

Virginia Blue Bells, Virginia Cowslip
- *Mertensia virginica* (L.) Pers. ex Link
- Borage family **Boraginaceae**

FLOWERING SEASON: mid-April to mid-May. FLOWERS: pale blue to bluish purple, several to many, in terminal clusters, about 1" (2.5 cm) long, trumpet-shaped, usually nodding. PLANT: 1–2' (30–60 cm) tall; leaves alternate, simple, oval, margin entire, green. HABITAT: moist meadows and woodlands.

Blue Toadflax
- *Linaria canadensis* (L.) Dumort
- Figwort family **Scrophulariaceae**

FLOWERING SEASON: May–September FLOWERS: pale blue, several to many, alternate in a slender terminal cluster, about ¼" (6 mm) long, tubular and 2-lipped with a hook-shaped slender spur at the base; upper lip with 2 erect petal-like lobes; lower lip with 3 larger, spreading, petal-like lobes. PLANT: 4–26" (10–65 cm) tall; leaves alternate, simple, long and narrow, margin entire, green. HABITAT: dry, often sandy, soil.

Butterwort / *Pinguicula vulgaris*

Virginia Blue Bells, Virginia Cowslip /
Mertensia virginica

Viper's Bugloss / *Echium vulgare*

Blue Toadflax / *Linaria canadensis*

Long-spurred Violet / *Viola rostrata*

Great Spurred Violet, Selkirk Violet /
Viola selkirkii

Dwarf Snapdragon
•*Chaenorrhinum minus* (L.) Lange
•Figwort family **Scrophulariaceae**
FLOWERING SEASON: July–August. FLOW-
ERS: lilac to pale blue, many, individual
flowers in leaf axils, about ¼" (6 mm)
long, tubular with a basal spur and 2 lips;
upper lip 2-lobed, lower lip 3-lobed.
PLANT: 6–12" (15–31 cm) tall; leaves
alternate, simple, narrowly oblong, margin entire, green. HABITAT: waste areas.

Great Blue Lobelia
•*Lobelia siphilitica* L.
•Bluebell family **Campanulaceae**
FLOWERING SEASON: August–September.
FLOWERS: bright blue, several to many in
a showy slender terminal cluster, up to 1"
(2.5 cm) long, tubular at the base, with 3
broad lower lobes and 2 smaller upper
lobes. PLANT: 1–3' (30–90 cm) tall;
leaves alternate, simple, lance-shaped,
margin toothed, green. HABITAT: moist
meadows, swamps, and edges of large
bodies of water.

Spiked Lobelia
•*Lobelia spicata* Lam.
•Bluebell family **Campanulaceae**
FLOWERING SEASON: July–August. FLOW-
ERS: pale blue, many in a slender terminal cluster, about ⁵⁄₁₆" (8 mm) long,
tubular and 2-lipped; upper lip with 2
narrow erect lobes; lower lip with 3
larger, lance-shaped lobes. PLANT: 1–4'
(0.3–1.2 m) tall; leaves alternate and
basal, simple, oblong to oval, margin
wavy, green. HABITAT: sandy soil along
woodlands and roadsides. COMMENTS:
brook lobelia, *Lobelia kalmii*, found in
moist soils along waterways, is pale blue
with a white central area on the lower
lip. Water lobelia, *L. dortmanna*, which
grows in shallow water, has pale blue or
whitish flowers and small basal leaves
that are frequently submerged.

Dayflower
•*Commelina communis* L.
•Dayflower family **Commelinaceae**
FLOWERING SEASON: July–September.
FLOWERS: blue, solitary to few, terminal, about ½" (1.3 cm) or more wide,
with 2 large, erect blue petals and a
smaller, whitish lower petal. PLANT:
erect or somewhat trailing, stems 1–3'
(30–90 cm) long; leaves alternate, simple,
broadly lance-shaped, margin entire,
green. HABITAT: waste areas and meadows.

LEAVES ALTERNATE, COMPOUND

Blue Columbine
•*Aquilegia vulgaris* L.
•Crowfoot family **Ranunculaceae**
FLOWERING SEASON: June. FLOWERS:
blue to purple, one to several, terminal,
about 1½" (3.8 cm) long with 5 tubular
petals, nodding. PLANT: 1–2' (30–60 cm)
tall; leaves alternate, compound with 3 to
9 leaflets; leaflets wedge-shaped and
irregularly lobed, green. HABITAT: woodlands, roadsides, and meadows.

Alfalfa
•*Medicago sativa* L.
•Bean family **Fabaceae**
FLOWERING SEASON: June–August.
FLOWERS: violet to blue, many, in
elongated clusters, about ¼" (6 mm)
long, narrowly pea-like. PLANT: 1–2'
(30–60 cm) tall; leaves alternate, compound with 3 leaflets; leaflets obovate,
margins minutely toothed near the tip,
green; fruit a cluster of brown, tightly
spiraled pods. HABITAT: fields, meadows, and waste areas.

Dayflower / *Commelina communis*

Spiked Lobelia / *Lobelia spicata*

Great Blue Lobelia / *Lobelia siphilitica*

Dwarf Snapdragon / *Chaenorrhinum minus*

Alfalfa / *Medicago sativa*

Blue Columbine / *Aquilegia vulgaris*

Cow-vetch
•*Vicia cracca* L.
•Bean family **Fabaceae**
FLOWERING SEASON: mid-June through July. FLOWERS: bluish purple, many, in 1–4" (2.5–10 cm) long, slender, 1-sided axial clusters, up to ½" (1.3 cm) long, narrowly pea-like, slightly nodding. PLANT: trailing vine, 2–4' (0.6–1.2 m) long; leaves alternate, pinnately compound with 18 to 24 leaflets; leaflets narrowly lance-shaped, margins entire, green. HABITAT: fields and waste areas.

Wild Lupine
•*Lupinus perennis* L.
•Bean family **Fabaceae**
FLOWERING SEASON: mid-May to mid-June. FLOWERS: bicolored, blue and white, sometimes pinkish, many in an erect cylindrical 6–10" (15–25 cm) tall terminal cluster, about ¾" (1.9 cm) long, pea-like. PLANT: 1–2' (30–60 cm) tall; leaves alternate, palmately compound with 7 to 11 leaflets; leaflets narrowly lance-shaped, margins entire, green. HABITAT: dry sandy soil.

LEAVES OPPOSITE, SIMPLE

Bottle Gentian, Closed Gentian
•*Gentiana clausa* Raf.
•Gentian family **Gentianaceae**
FLOWERING SEASON: mid-August to mid-September. FLOWERS: blue, several, usually in a terminal cluster, about 1½" (3.8 cm) long, corolla tubular, club-shaped to bottle-shaped, nearly to completely closed at the tip. PLANT: 1–2' (30–60 cm) tall; leaves usually opposite, often whorled in the upper 2 axils, simple, lance-shaped, margin entire, green. HABITAT: moist meadows and fens.

Common Skullcap
•*Scutellaria galericulata* L.
•Mint family **Lamiaceae**
FLOWERING SEASON: July–August. FLOWERS: blue, several, in pairs in axils, about 1" (2.5 cm) long, tubular, 2-lipped; upper lip hood-like and arched over the lower lip. PLANT: 1–3' (30–90 cm) tall; leaves opposite on a square stem, simple, lance-shaped, margin toothed, green. HABITAT: swamps and along streams. COMMENTS: 9 species of skullcaps have been reported from New York. Mad-dog skullcap, *Scutellaria lateriflora*, bears flowers in long, narrow axial clusters.

Gill-over-the-ground
•*Glechoma hederacea* L.
•Mint family **Lamiaceae**
FLOWERING SEASON: late April into July. FLOWERS: blue to violet, several, in axial clusters, about ¾" (1.9 cm) long, tubular with 2 lips; upper lip 2-lobed, lower lip 3-lobed. PLANT: prostrate, creeping, up to 18" (45 cm) long; leaves opposite on a square stem, simple, kidney-shaped, margin scalloped, green. HABITAT: waste areas, woods, thickets, and lawns.

Monkeyflower
•*Mimulus ringens* L.
•Figwort family **Scrophulariaceae**
FLOWERING SEASON: mid-July through August. FLOWERS: pale violet, few, axial, about 1" (2.5 cm) long, tubular with 2 spreading lips; upper lip with 2 petal-like lobes; lower lip with 3 rounded petal-like lobes. PLANT: 1–3' (60–90 cm) tall; leaves opposite on a square stem, simple, lance-shaped, margin toothed, green. HABITAT: swamps and along streams.

Bottle Gentian, Closed Gentian / *Gentiana clausa*

Wild Lupine / *Lupinus perennis*

Cow-vetch / *Vicia cracca*

Gill-over-the-ground / *Glechoma hederacea*

Common Skullcap / *Scutellaria galericulata*

Monkeyflower / *Mimulus ringens*

Bird's-eye Speedwell

•*Veronica persica* Poir.

•Figwort family **Scrophulariaceae**

FLOWERING SEASON: May–June. **FLOWERS:** a mixture of white and bluish purple with purple veining, many, axial, long-stalked, about 7/16" (1.1 cm) wide, tubular at the base, with 4 large, unequal, rounded, petal-like lobes. **PLANT:** often prostrate and forming mats; leaves opposite, simple, ovate, margin toothed, green. **HABITAT:** lawns, fields, and waste areas. **COMMENTS:** *Veronica chamaedrys*, also know as bird's-eye speedwell, has similar flowers, but they are borne on spike-like terminal clusters.

Bird's-eye Speedwell / *Veronica persica*

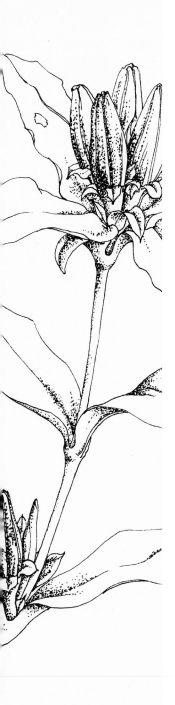

PART SIX

DARK PURPLE
TO BROWN FLOWERS

FLOWERS SYMMETRICAL, WITH 3 PETALS OR PETAL-LIKE PARTS

LEAVES BASAL, SIMPLE

Wild Ginger
•*Asarum canadense* L.
•Birthwort family **Aristolochiaceae**
FLOWERING SEASON: late April through
May. FLOWER: brownish purple, solitary,
axial, about 1" (2.5 cm) wide, tubular
with 3 narrowly triangular, petal-like
lobes, lying on or just above the ground.
PLANT: 6–12" (15–30 cm) tall; leaves
paired, appearing basal, simple, kidney-
shaped with a pointed tip, long-stalked,
margin entire, green. HABITAT: woodlands.

FLOWERS SYMMETRICAL, WITH 5 PETALS OR PETAL-LIKE PARTS

LEAVES MOSTLY OPPOSITE OR WHORLED, SIMPLE

Black Swallow-wort
•*Cynanchum louiseae* Kartesz & Gandhi
•Milkweed family **Asclepiadaceae**
FLOWERING SEASON: early June into July.
FLOWERS: dark purple, many, several in
loose axial clusters, about ¼" (6 mm)
wide, with 5 narrow, petal-like parts.
PLANT: twining and vine-like, 2–5'
(0.6–1.5 m) long; leaves mostly opposite,
simple, lance-shaped, margin entire,
green. HABITAT: variable (e.g., fields,
woodland edges and ravines). COM-
MENTS: often forms dense mats.

FLOWERS SYMMETRICAL, WITH 6 PETALS OR PETAL-LIKE PARTS

LEAVES OPPOSITE, COMPOUND

Blue Cohosh
•*Caulophyllum thalictroides* (L.) Michx.

•Barberry family **Berberidaceae**
FLOWERING SEASON: mid-April into May.
FLOWERS: greenish purple, brownish
purple, or yellowish green, several in
a loosely flowered cluster, up to ½"
(1.3 cm) wide, with 6 petal-like sepals.
PLANT: 1–3' (30–90 cm) tall; leaves opposite with 3 pinnately compound sections;
leaflets oval, 3 to 5 lobed, margin entire,
green. HABITAT: woodlands.

FLOWERS NOT RADIALLY SYM-METRICAL; FLOWERS MINUTE, OR WITH NO OBVIOUS PETAL-LIKE PARTS

TYPICAL LEAVES LACKING

Spotted Coralroot
•*Corallorhiza maculata* (Raf.) Raf.
•Orchid family **Orchidaceae**
FLOWERING SEASON: late July through
August. FLOWERS: greenish purple and
white with purple spots, 10 to 30 in a
slender terminal cluster on a purplish to
brownish stem, about ½" (1.3 cm) tall
and wide, with 5 greenish purple petals
and sepals and a white, purple-spotted
lip. PLANT: 8–16" (20–40 cm) tall; leaves
lacking. HABITAT: woodlands. COM-
MENTS: coralroots are indirect parasites
that feed on other plants. Early coralroot,
Corallorhiza trifida, which blooms in
June, is the only species with predomi-
nantly green coloration. Striped coralroot, *C. striata*, which has pinkish purple
stripes on the petal-like parts, blooms in
June, and, in New York, is only found in
one location. The autumn coralroot, *C.
odontorhiza*, which blooms in late August
through September, has tiny ⅛" (3 mm)
flowers that rarely open fully.

Blue Cohosh / *Caulophyllum thalictroides*

Wild Ginger / *Asarum canadense*

Black Swallow-wort / *Cynanchum louiseae*

Spotted Coralroot / *Corallorhiza maculata*

LEAVES BASAL, SIMPLE

Skunk-cabbage

•*Symplocarpus foetidus* (L.) Salisb. ex Nutt.
•Arum family **Araceae**
FLOWERING SEASON: March–April.
FLOWERS: minute, many on a globular cluster enclosed in a stiff 3–6" (7.5–15 cm) tall, firm, hood-shaped sheath that is purple-brown to greenish yellow and often mottled. **PLANT:** 1–2' (30–60 cm) tall; leaves basal, large, simple, broad with protruding veins like those of a cabbage, margin entire, green; unpleasant odor if bruised. **HABITAT:** swamps, moist soil. **COMMENTS:** the flowers, which emerge before the leaves, sometimes bloom through the snow.

LEAVES ALTERNATE, COMPOUND

Groundnut

•*Apios americana* Medik.
•Bean family **Fabaceae**
FLOWERING SEASON: August to mid-September. **FLOWERS:** brownish purple, many, in dense axial clusters, about ½" (1.3 cm) long, pea-like; fragrant. **PLANT:** vine-like, 3–8' (0.9–2.4 m) long; leaves alternate, pinnately compound with 5 to 7 leaflets; leaflets ovate, margins entire, green. **HABITAT:** moist thickets and meadows.

Skunk-cabbage / *Symplocarpus foetidus*

Groundnut / *Apios americana*

GLOSSARIES
AND INDEXES

❧

VISUAL GLOSSARY

Floral Parts

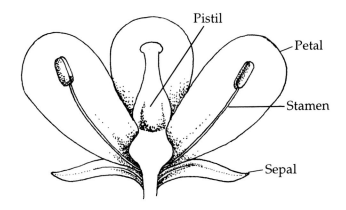

Pistil

Petal

Stamen

Sepal

Flower Types

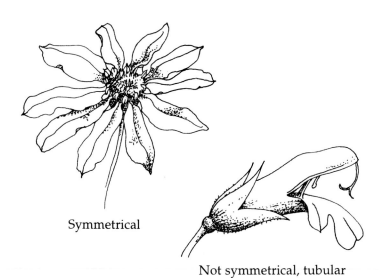

Symmetrical

Not symmetrical, tubular

Leaf Types

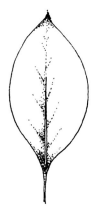

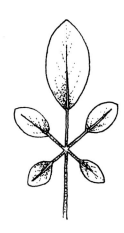

Simple   Pinnately compound   Palmately compound

Leaf Parts

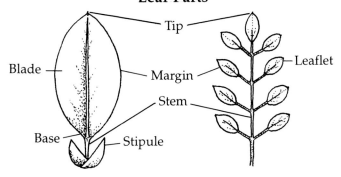

Tip

Blade

Margin

Leaflet

Stem

Base

Stipule

Leaf Arrangement

Opposite   Alternate   Whorled   Basal

Leaf Margins

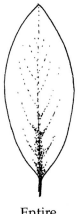 

Entire   Toothed   Lobed

Leaf Tips

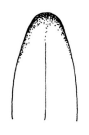  

Rounded, blunt   Tapered   Notched

Leaf/Petal Bases

Rounded   Tapered   Heart-shaped

GLOSSARY OF TERMS

ALTERNATE: having leaves arranged singly at different positions along the sides of the stem

APICAL: toward the tip

AXILLARY: located at a leaf-stem juncture

AXIS: the main stem

BASAL: located at the base

BOG: a wet, acidic, nutrient-poor peatland that relies on atmosphere sources for its moisture

BRACT: a small leaf-like structure

CALYX: the basal part of a flower that includes the sepals

COMPOUND: a leaf having two or more leaflets

COROLLA: the apical portion of a flower that includes the petals

DIOECIOUS: having male and female flowers on separate plants

ENDANGERED: referring to species having five or fewer sites, or fewer than 1,000 individuals known in New York State

ENTIRE: having a continuous margin unbroken by indentations or teeth

EVERGREEN: a plant retaining most of the leaves through the winter

FEN: a peatland that receives much of its moisture from ground water sources, typically less acidic and richer in nutrients than a true bog

FERTILE: being capable of sexual reproduction

HERBACEOUS: not woody

LEAFLET: one blade-like part of a compound leaf

LOBE: one part of a leaf or flower that is typically rounded

MARGIN: the edge

NODDING: bending downward

OBLANCEOLATE: pertaining to a leaf that is broadest near the tip

OBLONG: having sides nearly parallel and longer than broad

OBOVATE: egg-shaped, but with the broader end near the tip, the opposite of ovate

OPPOSITE: having leaves arranged in pairs on opposing sides of a stem

OVATE: shaped like an egg, with the broader end at the base

PALMATE: resembling a hand with spread fingers; in a leaf, having divisions radiating out from the center

PENDANT: suspended or hanging down

PERFOLIATE: pertaining to a leaf or leaves with the bases completely surrounding the stem and appearing to be pierced by it

PERIANTH: the combined term for the petals and sepals

PETAL: a usually colorful leaf-like part of the corolla

PINNATE: a leaf with leaflets arranged on opposite sides of the axis, resembling the divisions of a feather

PISTILLATE: referring to either a female flower or the female parts of a complete flower

PROSTRATE: lying flat on the ground

PUBESCENT: coated with short, soft hairs

RECURVED: curved backward or downward

RETICULATION: a net-like pattern

SEPAL: a leaf-like part of the calyx that may be either green or brightly colored

SESSILE: lacking a stalk

SIMPLE: pertaining to a leaf with a single undivided blade

SPATHULATE: shaped like a spoon

SPHERICAL: round or nearly so

SPUR: a tubular extension found on selected flower species, often containing nectar

STAMEN: the male or pollen-producing part of a flower

STAMINATE: referring to either a male flower or the male parts of a complete flower

STEM: the main axis that supports a plant

STERILE: not being capable of sexual reproduction

SWAMP: a wetland area typically containing woody vegetation

TERMINAL: located at the tip

THREATENED: referring to species having 6–19 sites, or fewer than 3,000 individuals known in New York State

TOMENTOSE: having soft matted hairs

TRUNCATE: cut off at one end

VEIN: a small enclosed channel in a leaf or petal through which nutrients and fluids pass

WASTE AREA: unutilized land typically in proximity to human habitation, frequently a site of organic wastes such as lawn clippings

WHORLED: having leaves arranged in groups of three or more around the same point on a stem

INDEX OF COMMON NAMES

INDEX OF GENERA AND SPECIES

WILLIAM K. CHAPMAN, a biology teacher and member of the adjunct faculty at Utica College of Syracuse University, is the author of *Orchids of the Northeast, Hickory, Chicory, and Dock* (a wild foods guide), *Plants and Flowers: An Archival Sourcebook, Pheasants under Glass,* and individual field guides to the trees, mammals, and birds of the Adirondacks. He is also a contributing author and photographer for *Deer: The Wildlife Series.* His nature photography has appeared in *National Geographic* and the *New York State Conservationist.*

VALERIE A. CHAPMAN is employed by Utica College of Syracuse University. Her photography has been published in *Birds of the Adirondacks* and *Mammals of the Adirondacks.* She enjoys travel, hiking, swimming, and beachcombing with her husband and two children, Andy and Carey.

ALAN E. BESSETTE is a mycologist and professor of biology at Utica College of Syracuse University. He is the author of *Edible and Poisonous Mushrooms of New York, Mushrooms of the Adirondacks* and coauthor of *Edible Wild Mushrooms of North America, Mushrooms of North America in Color: A Field Guide Companion to Seldom-Illustrated Fungi* (Syracuse University Press) and *Mushrooms of Northeastern North America* (Syracuse University Press). Alan has presented numerous mycological programs, is the scientific advisor to the Mid-York Mycological Society, and serves as a consultant for the New York State Poison Control Center. He was recipient of the 1992 North American Mycological Association Award for Contributions to Amateur Mycology.

ARLEEN R. BESSETTE is a mycologist and botanical photographer, as well as a psychologist, who has created and contributed over fifty original recipes for the book *Edible Wild Mushrooms of North America.* She is author of *Taming the Wild Mushroom: A Culinary Guide to Market Foraging* and coauthor of *Mushrooms of North American in Color: A Field Guide Companion to Seldom-Illustrated Fungi,* and *Mushrooms of Northeastern North America.* She has won several national awards for her photography and teaches workshops for the North American Mycological Association and the Northeastern Mycological Federation.

DOUGLAS R. PENS teaches ecology and biology at New Hartford High School, New Hartford, New York, and runs the school's Environmental Studies Program at Raquette Lake. He is also a teaching staff member with the Cornell Institute for Biology Teachers and Wildlife Rehabilitator for the State of New York specializing in hawks and owls. He is recipient of numerous awards, including the EPA's Environmental Achievement Award and the New York State Outstanding Biology Teacher Award, and was selected as a Tandy Technology Scholar. He resides in Clinton, New York, with his wife, Eileen, and children Amy, Chad, and Matt.